'Part autobiography, part travelogue, part spiritual journal, part theological reflection, this book is an entire treat! In it Maggi Dawn guides us to places both spatial and spiritual that we have never been before and helps us to see ourselves and the world around us with fresh eyes.'

– Paula Gooder, Canon Theologian of Birmingham
and Guildford Cathedrals and author of
This Risen Existence: The Spirit of Easter

'*The Accidental Pilgrim* is a welcome read for those of us who identify more with Chaucer's characters than the holier-than-thou crowd. Maggi Dawn's honest portrayals of her journey from tourist to pilgrim encourage me to keep walking along my own unique and crooked pilgrim path.'

– Becky Garrison, author of *Jesus Died For This?*
A Satirist's Search for the Risen Christ

'. . . [written] in a beautiful style that feels like a warm knife through butter.'

– *The United Church Observer*

'This lovely spiritual memoir of one woman's gradual discovery of what it means to be a pilgrim is an ideal companion for a new year.'

– *Woman Alive*

Also by Maggi Dawn

The Writing on the Wall

MAGGI DAWN

The Accidental Pilgrim

New journeys on ancient pathways

Leabharlanna Poiblí Chathair Baile Átha Cliath
Dublin City Public Libraries

HODDER

First published in Great Britain in 2011 by Hodder & Stoughton
An Hachette UK company
This paperback edition first published in 2012

2

A CIP catalogue record for this title is available from the British Library

ISBN 978 0 340 98006 4
eBook ISBN 978 1 444 70299 6

Typeset in New Baskerville by Hewer Text UK Ltd, Edinburgh

Printed and bound in the UK by CPI Group (UK) Ltd, Croydon, CR0 4YY

Hodder & Stoughton policy is to use papers that are natural, renewable
and recyclable products and made from wood grown in sustainable
forests. The logging and manufacturing processes are expected to
conform to the environmental regulations of the country of origin.

Hodder & Stoughton Ltd
338 Euston Road
London NW1 3BH

www.hodderfaith.com

Writing this book has made me more grateful
than ever for the many people who have helped
to shape my life, but in particular for those who
both taught and befriended me as I unravelled my
faith and put it back together again in Cambridge
– especially Graham Davies, Janet Soskice, Jeremy
Begbie and Jane Keiller. Without them I would
never have become any kind of pilgrim at all.

Contents

1

Accidental pilgrim

Life's a voyage that's homeward bound.
Herman Melville, novelist and sailor (1819–91)

Standing on the cool, bare tiles in the shade of the wooden shutters at the window, I squinted into the bright light. Directly below was a military checkpoint, and to either side the road was lined with tumbledown buildings. Beyond them the sandy landscape was cobwebbed with olive trees and far away in the distance some new buildings on the upper slopes of the hills shone dazzling white in the late afternoon sun. In the shade of my room, my few clothes hung in the cupboard, my backpack was stowed away and my notebooks sat in a neat pile on the small desk next to a polite notice warning guests not to drink the water from the bathroom taps.

There was an hour until supper – too long to do nothing, but not enough time to get very far afield. Then came a soft knock at the door, and Rudy's shaggy head appeared.

'Settled in, then?' he said.

'Didn't take long.'

'I know what you mean,' he said, looking round. 'My room is a carbon copy of yours. So – did you feel it, then, the mystical thing when your feet touched the tarmac?'

'Don't be daft.'

'What, no spiritual feelings at all? No magical sense that God is here?'

'Give me a break. No – wait – don't tell me *you* had an epiphany?'

Rudy laughed. 'In an airport? I can't imagine a less likely place for a revelation. Anyway, never mind all that. Let's go for a walk before supper and check the place out.'

We left the cool room, walked through long, neatly swept corridors to the main door of the college, and stepped out into the gardens. The heat rose from the sun-baked ground, and the air was redolent with the sweet smell of rosemary bushes, mixed with the promising aroma of baking bread wafting from the kitchens. The college lay a couple of miles outside Jerusalem on the road to Bethlehem, and was to be the base from which we would spend the coming weeks on a study tour of the Holy Land. The next morning we would meet our guide, but for this evening all we had to do was eat, sleep and meet the others on the trip – thirty or so students from universities and colleges all over the UK.

☞

Rudy and I had just completed our second year studying theology at Cambridge. I was at Fitzwilliam, which had been founded in the nineteenth century as a society for young men from artisan families who lacked sufficient money to enter a college. By the time I arrived at Fitz, it had long since become established as a college within the university, but was still proud of the fact that it led the way in making Cambridge accessible to the brightest sons of the London Guilds.

The students were no less bright in the 1990s. Fresh from the rigours of school and awesomely well read, they all seemed accomplished, polished and confident. As a mature student embarking on my degree after a first career in the music industry, I had felt slightly the odd one out – and not having written an essay in more than a decade, I had spent my first year working ferociously hard, afraid I wouldn't keep up. My motivation gradually shifted, though, as I discovered a sheer love of the subject, reading my way through Augustine and Athanasius, Freud and Jung, Darwin and Coleridge, Wittgenstein and Rahner. I learned to read the Bible in Greek, found out that some of its stories date right back to the Bronze Age, that parts of it had been rewritten several times over, that its many authors wrote from entirely different perspectives, that it doesn't appear in the order in which it was written, and that you can trace within its pages a development of the idea of 'God' from one era to another. Academic theology, then, turned out to be nothing like its vaguely mystical and outdated caricature: I found myself in the midst of a rigorous intellectual endeavour where no stone was left unturned, and there was no question that couldn't be asked. If I found God anywhere in Cambridge, it was in the library and the lecture hall rather than the chapel.

The Faculty of Divinity in those days was housed in a somewhat Gothic red-brick building opposite St John's College, and Fitz was too far away to nip back for a cup of tea between lectures. Rudy, though, had a riverside room at St John's, just a stone's throw from the faculty, and our friendship began with his offer of tea between lectures. Rudy was almost a decade younger than me, had a posh accent and came from a wealthy background. He looked like a bit of a hippy with his floppy hair, but was actually pretty conservative, more likely to be found in the tea room of an art gallery than a nightclub. We had little in common apart from an interest in theology and a love of art, but we quickly slipped into an easy and uncomplicated friendship which (though we didn't know it at the time) would last way beyond university.

As our second year drew to a close, I went for my last supervision of the term with a young lecturer who taught New Testament.

'I hear you're going on a study tour,' he said as the supervision ended. 'Have you ever been to Israel before?'

'Nope,' I said. 'Of the various bits of the Bible landscape, I've seen Egypt and Greece, but never Israel.'

'You'll love it,' said my lecturer confidently. 'I go there every chance I get. It's not only that you get to understand your work in a new way. There's just something different about it.'

'I know what you mean,' I said. 'I've stood on the place where they fought the Battle of Hastings, and where Custer made his last stand, and on the road where Kennedy was assassinated. It's a magic feeling being right on the spot – brings history to life.'

'Yeah,' he replied, 'but I'm not just talking about history. I mean something spiritual. You walk on the same ground that Jesus did, and suddenly you feel that God is there. I can't explain it – it's not rational. But even as you set your foot on the ground, you'll feel it.'

I was astonished to hear this from a man who had spent the last two years pulling me up on every detail of thought, every failure of logic, every slip of rational thinking. There was no room in an essay for unvarnished personal opinion or subjective belief; everything had to be accounted for, the facts backed up with evidence, the argument watertight. How could he now be sending me off on a study tour, telling me to expect a mystical experience?

'You mean the very moment you step out of the plane?' I tried to cover my cynicism with a joke. 'I don't think the tarmac was there when Jesus was around . . .'

He smiled. 'I'll be in Jerusalem in the last week of your trip,' he said. 'Meet me for tea, and tell me whether I'm right or not.'

≈

I remembered his words as the plane touched down at Ben Gurion airport, thinking that it wouldn't need an epiphany to make this trip fantastic: long, sunny days poking around in archaeological sites already sounded like heaven to me. As we emerged from the cabin doors, the heat was like opening an oven door, and at the bottom of the steps the ground had the smell and the faint softness of hot tarmac.

Hand luggage in one hand and passport in the other, I thought of the millions of other travellers who had made their way here over the centuries – tourists, exiles, pilgrims, nomads, crusaders. Back in the mists of time Abraham and his family had wandered in and out of this land, and later small tribes had come down from the hills, or followed Moses through the desert to find their Promised Land of milk and honey. Their descendants built the ancient city of Jerusalem more than five thousand years ago, since when it has been besieged, attacked, captured and recaptured repeatedly, and twice almost completely destroyed. The Babylonians razed the city to the ground in 586 BC, and many of the Jews were taken into exile for eighty years, after which their sons and daughters returned and rebuilt the city. Over the ruins of Solomon's Temple a second Temple was constructed, but it took so long to build that the final details were barely complete before the Romans destroyed the city again in AD 70. By that time Christianity was in its infancy and both Jews and Christians, aware that serious trouble was brewing, had begun to flee Jerusalem to find safe harbour. And a few centuries later Jerusalem was the target for a new round of conflicts as three world religions laid claim to it. As far back as human memory extends, then, this Holy Land has seen a constant flow in and out of people with clashing political and religious identities, struggling for its ownership, and making it as much an icon of bloody conflict as of holiness.

Outside the airport we caught the bus to Jerusalem. We passed roadside cafés where people relaxed over coffee, shops with brilliantly coloured displays of fresh fruit and split watermelons, and row upon row of lush orange groves, lemon trees and date farms. It wasn't hard to see why this little slip of land between coastline and desert should have been seen in ancient times as a gift from God, a land of milk and honey, worth fighting over time and again. But whether, as my lecturer had suggested, the presence of God still somehow mystically resided there, it would be interesting to see. I jotted a few lines and some sketches in my notebook and reminded myself that I was here to study, not embark on a pilgrimage.

After supper on that first evening the members of the tour were gathered for formal introductions. Most of them were not just studying theology, but were also in training for professional ministry and were carving out their religious identity, some more self-consciously than others. A young man of about twenty-two had just embarked on his degree in a college training Roman Catholic priests. Tall, good-looking and rather vain, he drank like a fish, wore a clerical collar at all times and styled himself as 'Father', despite the fact that he wasn't going to be a priest for at least seven years yet. A young woman could barely articulate her feelings about arriving in Israel, mentioned the word 'pilgrimage' a couple of times and burst into helpless sobs. Another man didn't talk much about religion at all, but spoke of how growing up amid the Troubles of Northern Ireland coloured his view both of biblical history and of current Middle Eastern conflicts. And, as in most religious gatherings, there was a pair of irritatingly over-keen evangelists who seemed to think that their God-given role on this trip was to correct everyone else's point of view, interspersing every conversation with somewhat Pharisaical interjections about the 'true meaning' of the Bible. Several other members of the tour introduced themselves as 'just' partners and spouses, along for the adventure, and I couldn't help thinking that as they had the fewest expectations they might turn out to have the most interesting time. Anthony Burgess famously remarked about Rome, the second great pilgrimage destination, 'All of human life is here . . .' and it didn't seem a bad description of the assortment of pilgrims, scholars, evangelists, politicos and tourists who were setting out on this trip.

I wasn't sure I wanted to be referred to as a pilgrim, but then I remembered Chaucer's motley crew of companions and their assorted backgrounds and motivations. When Chaucer wrote *The Canterbury Tales* between 1387 and 1400, pilgrimage was at the height of its popularity and was valued as much as an excuse for travel and entertainment, or to make business, social or romantic connections, as for its religious purposes. Chaucer's entire company of pilgrims, including – or perhaps especially – the professionally religious ones, had mixed motives. The most deeply corrupt were the Pardoner and the Summoner, both of whom had secular roles within the Church, but even the Monk and the Prioress failed to exhibit any kind of spiritual depth, being more preoccupied with expensive clothes and other luxuries, and indulging in a little flirtation here and there. The most morally upright was the chivalrous Knight, who was clearly admired both by the Host and the Narrator, yet Chaucer didn't sanitise him into an infallible hero, but allowed the bawdy, unsophisticated Miller to show up the weaknesses of his chivalrous ideology. The women on the pilgrimage are equally believable characters. The Wife of Bath was a savvy and experienced traveller who had already visited five other

European pilgrim sites. Famously married five times, she was clearly a sexy woman who enjoyed her physical pleasures, but also smart enough to make the most of the economic benefits of marriage. And the Nun, seemingly so spiritual, gradually revealed herself to be rather more vain and fond of trinkets and luxuries than suited her profession. Of all the pilgrims, the only one who seemed purely spiritual in intent was the Second Nun. By making each pilgrim a mix of good and bad, rather than giving them typecast roles, Chaucer created characters that still come off the page, laughing, joking and provoking each other over everything from the utmost seriousness to ribald humour, so that the focus of the narrative is the pilgrims themselves rather than their destination.

Six centuries later, on a hot evening in Jerusalem, it struck me that for all the enormous advances since Chaucer's day, his ability to put his finger on the vagaries of human nature with such wit and affection had a timeless quality to it. We too were a company of travellers setting out on our journey with various expectations and highly mixed motives. Some of our company who described themselves as 'mere' tourists had also expressed the hope of encountering God's presence in the land where Jesus himself had walked, while one or two of the most self-consciously religious among the group were looking forward to a bit of a holiday from the rigours of their closeted institutions. As for me, I had set out absorbed in my own idea of a scholarly adventure without giving too much thought to the people I would meet along the way. As the evening's conversation continued, liberally peppered with

9

the words 'pilgrimage' and 'holiday', I began to realise that their expectations of the trip would impinge on my own.

The next morning we met Joe, our guide, a wiry little man with red hair who lived and breathed biblical history. He began with an introductory lecture, and then went on to give us plenty of hints on getting the most out of a trip to a dig, surviving the desert without getting sunburnt or dehydrated, and how to get about without offending the locals. And then we were off into the middle of Jerusalem where, cheek by jowl with the buzz and business of modern life, lay the ruins of the ancient city. Around every corner was a dig, or a site of religious significance – here the foundations of the Temple, there the city wall that had first been built by David and Solomon and later repaired by Ezra and Nehemiah, and in between, built into the hillside, the remains of the homes of first-century priests and artisans – layers and layers of history within just a few square miles. Whole days were eaten up as we walked from one site to another, stopping in each place for a mini-lecture from our guide on the archaeological and geographical features, and the cultural and historical context that made sense of the biblical stories of the ancient kings and prophets of Israel, and of Jesus and his disciples. In the central areas – the Temple Mount, the Via Dolorosa, the Church of the Holy Sepulchre – and among the olive groves on the hillsides around the city, significant moments in biblical history were illuminated as we studied the geography and the archaeological remains.

Growing up in England, I had always taken it for granted that wherever you turn you find yourself standing on a place of significance. Within the confines of one small island you can see the remains of Stone Age, Bronze Age and Iron Age settlements, walk for miles along a wall built by the Romans, retrace the steps of the Battle of Hastings, or sit in seats built for Tudor kings. And on any weekend of the year you can find a reconstruction of some historical event or era at a castle, battlefield or stately home. Travelling around Israel is similarly densely packed with history – not only the ancient history of biblical times, but also the struggles of more recent centuries. The scars left by the Crusades are there to be seen, the heartbreaking tragedies of the Holocaust are presented neatly at Yad Vashem, while the untidy rubble of more recent and unresolved conflicts litters some of the areas that most tourists don't see. And right in the middle the Temple Mount, now equally claimed by the three religions of the book as foundational to their history, stands as a stark reminder that these apparently modern politico-religious struggles are, in fact, far more ancient and complex than they first seem. Not for nothing has this land been called the navel of the world.

On our tour around the city, though, we stopped not only at the ruins of ancient city walls and dwellings, but also at churches and chapels from the Byzantine to the modern era, built to commemorate the historical moments associated with the place. The overlay of centuries of Church history sometimes obscured the ancient themes, and sometimes were interesting in their own right, but listening to Joe's lectures at each stop we began to piece together not only a picture of biblical history, but also the history of Christianity, Judaism and Islam. Jesus, of course, was mentioned over and over again, along with the various heroes and villains of the Bible – David, Solomon, Herod, Judas, Mary Magdalene, Peter, Paul – but in addition to these one other name in particular was mentioned repeatedly as we went from one site to another: that of Helena, the mother of Constantine.

Just before going into battle with his enemy Maxentius at Milvian Bridge in the year 312, the Roman Emperor Constantine the Great is said to have had a dream in which he saw the *chi-rho* cross – the first two letters of the Greek word for 'Christ', which resemble an English X and P. Waking from his dream, he ordered *chi-rho* to be inscribed as his monogram on his army's standard and shields, and when a decisive victory followed, Constantine attributed his success to the God of the Christians. Not long afterwards he eased the situation of Christians by granting freedom of religion in his empire, and another decade later he became the first Roman emperor formally to adopt Christianity. Constantine's conversion had a dramatic impact on Christians, not only by ending the horrifying persecutions they had suffered under Diocletian, but also by encouraging the development of pilgrimage, because of his mother Helena's interest in sacred spaces.

Helena had grown up as an innkeeper until she became the consort of Constantius, Constantine's father. He later abandoned her to marry a younger woman, but Constantine held his mother in great affection, and she quickly followed him as a Christian convert, bringing with her the Greco-Roman tradition of travelling to sacred places to invoke the gods. After her conversion, Helena travelled to Jerusalem to search for the remains of the wooden cross on which Jesus had been crucified, and then took it upon herself to identify as many places as possible that were directly connected to significant moments in the life of Jesus. Such concern for artefacts and important geographical monuments had not been typical of Christianity up to that point, but Helena and Constantine built three grand monuments to Jesus in the Holy Land: the Church of the Holy Sepulchre on the site where he was crucified, the Church of the Nativity in Bethlehem over the cave where he was born, and a third basilica, the Church of Eleona, on the Mount of Olives at the place where he is said to have prophesied the destruction of Jerusalem – and also, by tradition, where he taught his disciples the Lord's Prayer. Once Helena had found what she believed to be the true cross, pilgrimage to Jerusalem began to grow, one of the earliest records being that of 'The Bordeaux Pilgrim' who travelled from Bordeaux via Milan, Constantinople, Tripoli, Beirut, Sidon and Tyre, arriving in Jerusalem in AD 333. Despite having made this enormous journey, he did not continue the relatively short distance beyond Jerusalem to Galilee.[1] For the early pilgrims, the importance of Jesus' passion and death far outweighed the geography of his early ministry.

Helena's dedication to marking the significant sites began a trend that continued through the centuries, and thus it was that our first week walking around Jerusalem included many visits to chapels, shrines and monuments as well as archaeological digs. It was a combination that seemed to be haunted by a particular disjunction. At every site we visited, Joe would begin by explaining the connection between the place and the particular slice of biblical history to which it related – whether that was as ancient as King David, some ten centuries BC, or the stories of Jesus, or some later event in Christian, Jewish or Islamic history. Some places, like the ancient walls of the city of David, or Hezekiah's Tunnel,[2] belonged unmistakably to particular accounts, while others were traditional memorial sites whose significance had been created later through the practice of pilgrimage.

Modern-day pilgrims were in evidence wherever we went; like us, they were touring the religious and historical landscape, but rather than notebooks they carried rosaries, hymn sheets and prayer books. There were countless occasions when we would wait for these groups to pray and sing their way through various rituals before we took our turn to study the site we had come to see. As we waited and watched the different rituals of groups from all over the world, I contemplated the different ways you can approach a place that has historical and cultural significance. For me, the trip had a clear purpose – I wanted to gain knowledge that went beyond information gleaned from books. I wanted to know this place, to feel the sense of the stories in my imagination in a way that is hard to access without feeling the intensity of the heat, eating the food of the region, encountering the sounds and smells of the culture. But for the pilgrim groups, they seemed to arrive with the expectation that they would encounter God himself: that being in the place where Jesus was born might open the way for some kind of spiritual rebirth; that visiting the Pool of Siloam where Jesus reportedly healed a paralysed man, they too might find some kind of healing. Our scholarly adventure followed in the footsteps of worshippers who seemed to care little about the authenticity of the place; their interest, as they clutched at prayer beads, or sang with arms raised to heaven, was in an encounter with their God.

Nowhere was this more apparent than at the site of Helena's first project, the Church of the Holy Sepulchre, by tradition the place where Jesus was crucified, buried and later resurrected. Here several different denominations occupy various corners of the building, each one with their own particular claim on Christian history – the largest denomination, the oldest, or the one that speaks Jesus' original language. It's hard to decide whether the shared space speaks of the triumph of unity or the irony that even in the place that most symbolises belief in a loving and reconciling God, people still remain divided. At the centre where the tomb itself lies there is a profusion of candles, lights and symbols of the different strands of Christianity from around the world. The overall effect of this most holy of sites is of a fabulously cluttered space where every group wants to hang its particular oil lamp, logo or devotional paraphernalia. We queued for a long time before being admitted for the briefest of visits to the tomb itself, all the time being waved through by a nun whose task it was to keep the queue moving like a slow airport escalator – a task she fulfilled with all the unsympathetic brusqueness of a high school gym teacher. A few pilgrims broke out of line to kneel and pray at the tomb, but apart from a few in the clothes of religious orders, none were allowed more than a few seconds to touch the holy place.

The clutter, the confusion, the queue, the moving crowd and the bossy nun all made what should have been a holy moment a bit of a circus: no time to reflect or pray, or even to think – just a hasty, supervised walk through.

Later in the day Joe led the way up to a quiet hillside. At first it wasn't apparent what we had come to see, but then he pointed to a little wrinkle in the landscape, and as we drew closer we saw a hillside tomb dating from the first or second century. The opening stood about four feet high, and halfway across the mouth of the tomb was a large stone disc, about the size and shape of a large millstone, which could be rolled in either direction to open or close the tomb. 'This is definitely *not* the tomb Jesus was buried in,' said Joe. 'But it does gives you a far clearer impression of what his tomb would have looked like than what we saw this morning.'

We walked inside the tomb and out again, gaining some sense of what a first-century burial was like: the cool, dark interior of the tomb, which seemed like a small room, and two long low stone shelves inside like twin beds on either side of the tomb, where the wrapped bodies would have been laid. After the crowds of pilgrims and the chaotic sights and smells of the Church of the Holy Sepulchre, it seemed far easier to visualise the events of Jesus' death up here on the remote hillside at the tomb of some unknown, unnamed people.

Tombs became something of a feature that week, for the following day, on the slopes of the Mount of Olives, we visited the oldest Jewish cemetery in the world to be in continuous use. For centuries Jews wanted to be buried there because it was directly above the Golden Gate, through which it was believed that the Messiah would return and those resurrected from the dead would be the first to follow him into the city. Further up the hill is Bethany, where Jesus raised Lazarus from the dead in a prophetic sign of his own forthcoming resurrection, and close to the summit the site of the ascension of the risen Christ. By both Jewish and Christian tradition, then, the Mount of Olives is iconic of life, death and future resurrection.

Later the same day we were back in the city, standing at the top of the enormous steps outside the Temple.

'Sit down, everyone, I want to show you something,' said Joe.

Grateful for the rest, we sat on the steps and drank from our water bottles as he walked five or six steps further down. Then he turned and began to quote from memory the words of Jesus from St Matthew's Gospel. Acting the part, and using plenty of hand gestures, he looked for all the world like a real live preacher, and a few bystanders stopped to see what the lecture would be about. But this was not a sermon of peace and love. 'Woe to you,' yelled Joe, pointing an accusing finger at us as he slipped into role and quoted some of the more brusque words of Jesus, startling a group of bystanders and intriguing us with what new drama this was. 'Woe to you,' he shouted, 'teachers of the law and Pharisees, you hypocrites! You are like whitewashed tombs, which look beautiful on the outside but on the inside are full of the bones of the dead and everything unclean' (Matt. 23:27).

Joe's performance made it easy to see that the natural theatre of the Temple steps was the perfect spot for Jesus to preach, and we were easily transported back to the scene. But the startled onlookers made me wonder why, of all the words of Jesus he could have chosen, Joe had picked that particular bit of invective against the hypocrisy of the religious leaders of the time. Jesus told some pretty comforting stories as well as speaking his mind to his enemies – why not a nice parable or two? But then I noticed he was looking pointedly over to our left, and followed his gaze across the Kidron Valley to the Mount of Olives. There in the near distance were the very tombs we had visited that morning. It only took a little imagination to realise that, freshly whitewashed, they would have gleamed in the sunlight. Jesus wasn't just picking any random metaphor – he was using the landscape as a visual aid.

Jesus' harsh words to the Pharisees are sometimes quoted to reinforce the idea that he was interested in spirituality, but against organised religion. Yet the picture is not quite as simple as that. From what we can trace through the Gospels, Jesus certainly criticised hypocrisy, corruption and the use of religious power for personal ends, but he also spent a lot of time and effort joining in with the religious practices of his time – visiting the Temple, attending synagogue and taking part in various feasts. It was only in Jerusalem, though, that the penny dropped for me that Jesus had himself also taken part in pilgrimages. Later in the week we returned to the Mount of Olives to follow the route of Jesus' entry into Jerusalem a few days before his death. Jesus is known to have stayed regularly in Bethany with his friends Lazarus, Martha and Mary, and Bethphage was a little further up the hill, and it was from here that the Palm Sunday procession began.

Looking back from the perspective of Christian history, it might appear that the crowds of people turned up specially to welcome Jesus into Jerusalem, but it's thought that on the first Palm Sunday Jesus and his disciples joined an existing pilgrimage into Jerusalem, which every year marked the hope of the long-awaited Messiah. It was only as the procession moved down the hill that Jesus gradually became the centre of attention.

We followed the likely route of the pilgrimage, starting at Bethphage and stopping en route at the place where Jesus is said to have stood and wept over Jerusalem (Luke 19:41). Dominus Flevit, the church built at this place, offers one of the most famous views of Jerusalem through its unglazed wrought-iron window.

Walking down the slopes, I pictured Jesus on the pilgrimage procession that became woven in with the story of that last week of his life, and began to think I might pay more attention to the next group of pilgrims we encountered. I didn't have long to wait.

Further down the hill we stopped at the site of the Church of Eleona, the third basilica Helena and Constantine had erected in honour of Jesus. This is supposedly the place where Jesus first taught his disciples the Lord's Prayer:

> Our Father in heaven,
> hallowed be your name,
> your kingdom come,
> your will be done,
> on earth as it is in heaven.

> Give us today our daily bread.
> And forgive us our debts,
> as we also have forgiven our debtors.
> And lead us not into temptation,
> but deliver us from the evil one.
> (Matt. 6:9–13)

Helena's Byzantine structure was destroyed by the Persians in AD 614, and apart from some of the foundation stones and some pillar bases, there isn't much left to see. Even less survived of its replacement, Pater Noster, a crusader chapel that was eventually destroyed, it's thought, by Saladin's forces in 1187. Centuries later a building project was begun by the French, only to be abandoned in 1927 when funds ran out. Nearby, though, stands a small convent; this was bought in 1868 by an Italian aristocrat called Aurelia Bossie who married into the French royalty and was persuaded into her investment by Marie Alphonse Ratisbonne, a French Jew and Christian convert. The convent was extended and the walls of the chapel and cloisters decorated with ceramic tiles on which the Lord's Prayer is painted in 140 different languages.

The cloisters were quiet when we arrived, and there was plenty to ponder: the dozens of languages were a testament to the extent of Christianity's influence, while a few yards away the various churches that had been erected and then destroyed witnessed to the conflict and competition that religion some-times engenders. I was aware that this site had more to do with the pilgrimage tradition than with biblical history. There's no clear evidence to tie Jesus' teaching on prayer to this particular place; one hillside olive grove looks pretty much like another, and the teachings could have been given anywhere from here to the Sea of Galilee. What's more, some biblical scholars think that, rather than being a prayer he taught his disciples to recite, the Lord's Prayer is really a conglomeration of Jesus' teachings from different occasions.

I was taught to recite the Lord's Prayer and the Apostles' Creed in Sunday school as a child, and as being word perfect was the prerequisite to being accepted for confirmation, I learned them much as I learned a piece of poetry or my times tables: it was a job to be done, and what it meant mattered far less than whether I got the words right. This was rather far removed from the story Matthew and Luke tell, of Jesus' followers being so amazed at his radical ideas, personal charisma and spiritual conviction that they longed to know what was the secret of his relationship to God. What words did Jesus use when he went off by himself to pray through the night? What did he know about praying that they didn't? When they said, 'Teach us to pray, Lord,' I don't think they were politely asking for the next bit of their catechism, or for a form of words. I think they were desperate to know the key to the connection he seemed to make between heaven and earth.

The cloisters were a pleasant, shady spot to ponder the meaning of prayer. But just then a large, air-conditioned coach pulled up outside the door, and we were interrupted by yet another group of pilgrims. Tranquillity vanished as nearly fifty more people jostled into the building. Wide eyed and excited, they listened for a few moments to their priest who spoke very fast in Spanish, and then, absolutely in sync, the whole group closed their eyes, raised their hands to the sky and began praying, not only in Spanish but in a babble of ecstatic speech, cries and moans. Disregarding the presence of others around them, the volume of their praying rose and their emotions swelled until several of them sank to their knees, praying and crying, tears streaming down their faces.

Up till that moment it hadn't seemed too difficult for various groups of pilgrims, students and tourists to accommodate each other. With a bit of mutual respect and patience there was generally enough room for everyone, and there seemed to be an unspoken agreement that people would wait for one group to finish before the next group filled the space. But the complete self-absorption of this group seemed strikingly out of alignment with the words written all around the walls. Didn't *Our Father* suggest to them that they might treat fellow visitors with a bit of respect? *Thy kingdom come on earth*? Getting pushed into a corner by people who seemed to think they had a prior claim on holy spaces didn't feel like heaven on earth to me. But then my indignation receded as I thought of the words *as we forgive those who sin against us*, and I decided I'd better get off my high horse and give them some space. Leaving the cacophony behind, I walked back to the ruins of Helena's chapel, which suddenly seemed to me less a record of history and more a monument to our repeated human failure to forgive and accommodate one another.

Looking behind me, I caught sight of the noisy pilgrims dashing back to their bus, handbags flying and loud exclamations filling the air. But a little further down the slope the olive grove was devoid of tourists, pilgrims or students, the only people in sight being some olive farmers a few hundred yards below. Sitting in the shade of an olive tree, I thought more about prayer and the noisy pilgrims I had just encountered. Was that really what pilgrimage was about? How did arriving in an air-conditioned coach and spending less than ten minutes looking at their destination inspire such an ecstatic experience? There was no attraction for me in a religion that made people oblivious to those around them, or a mystical experience that could apparently be summoned up at will and then turned off again without a second thought. But for some reason I couldn't quite fathom, the encounter had really bothered me. Perhaps my consternation was less to do with other people's religion than with an uncertainty about my own. I loved the historical jigsaw puzzle and the ancient poetry of the biblical texts, and I wanted to live by the high ideals of Jesus' teaching, but I disliked intensely some of the traditions that had accrued around the Christian faith like so many barnacles on the side of a boat, traditions that seemed to me neither to deepen nor to clarify faith, but to obscure it altogether. The dark, incense-laden interiors of many of the chapels we had visited, while interesting enough as historical records, did nothing to touch my soul. But sitting under an olive tree, I found it easy to picture Jesus hanging out with his disciples, and their voices seemed to sound down the centuries. 'Lord, teach us to pray,' they had begged him. But what I really wanted to say was, 'Lord, if praying is nothing more than a religious observance, then *don't* teach me to pray. I don't want to take part in affected religiosity or fakery or emotional manipulation. I'd rather be an agnostic and be genuine about it.'

The cloisters, for me, had opened windows onto history but lacked any sense of the numinous. But in the peaceful ordinariness of the olive grove there was that sense that time stood still. A slight breeze moved the heavy air, the crickets chirped, and far down the slopes the farmers called out to each other as they set their olive nets. It almost felt as if, had I turned round, I might have seen Jesus right there on the hillside, amused at my being hot and bothered over other people's religion. My sense of humour began to recover, and inwardly I made my peace with the noisy, annoying pilgrims. Suddenly I jumped up: how long had I been sitting here, musing to myself? I must have been there half an hour, and the group would have moved on without me. I ran back up the slope, and was amazed to find that I'd been in the olive grove for less than ten minutes.

An hour later I was heading back to the college for supper. The blue-and-white buses that travelled from Jerusalem down the Bethlehem road were hot and crowded. I shut my eyes and tried to summon up a clear idea of what pilgrimage was. I thought of childhood walks along the Pilgrims Way in southern England, and of the wrinkled fingers and toes I'd seen preserved in the reliquary at the Duomo Museum in Florence. I remembered pictures of people waiting in line at the shrine at Lourdes and hoping for a healing, and of scores of people painfully ascending steps in Rome on their knees. I thought of the hilarious and irreverent stories that Chaucer's pilgrims told to pass the time on their lengthy journey in *The Canterbury*

Tales, of Jesus' portentous pilgrimage down the Mount of Olives towards Jerusalem, and of the intense experience of medieval pilgrims such as Ignatius of Loyola and Margery Kempe who had to overcome all kinds of obstacles to realise their dream. Seeing real live pilgrims up close brought it home to me that my view of pilgrimage was a scattered collection of images like random pieces from a jigsaw with most of the bits missing and no picture on the box to help put them together. Was pilgrimage really about the journey or the destination? Did it matter whether the destination had any historical verification, or was it entirely a matter of tradition, or even superstition? Were pilgrims supposed to suffer penances, or – like Chaucer's pilgrims or the pilgrims on the tourist coach – was a pilgrimage equally valid made in comfort? What did people expect from pilgrimage: healing, spiritual enlightenment or the promise of heaven? I made a mental note to find out more, and to fill in the gaps in my knowledge.

⟋

The next phase of our trip was notable for the complete absence of pilgrims. We boarded a bus and drove into the desert, where most of the sites we visited were principally of interest to historians and archaeologists. We were somewhat mystified by our first stop. Looking around, there seemed to be nothing but a dusty track winding through a small gorge between two expanses of sandy hills. We weren't far enough south to be following Moses' journey through the wilderness, so we wondered whether we were about to be given a lesson on Jesus' temptations. But with no stones, no dig and no commemorative chapel to give us any clues, we had to wait for Joe to reveal the reason why he had brought us to this particular place.

For ten minutes or so we followed him along the track, going down a slight decline. Turning a corner, the track flattened out, by which time our transport was far out of sight. The sun was baking hot and despite being in a slight dip there was precious little shade to be found, and the light was so intense that even with sunglasses and hats we squinted uncomfortably. At last Joe stopped and we gathered round him to find out what we were doing in the middle of nowhere.

'This is the old road from Jericho to Jerusalem,' he began. 'When Jesus told the story of the Good Samaritan, this is what would have come to mind. Look around you. No shade, no relief from the beating sun. But the small hills that rise on each side of the road are full of hiding places where bandits lived. This was a dangerous road to travel – people would generally avoid travelling alone, particularly if they were carrying any goods with them. If you were attacked and robbed on this road in the midday heat, and left without water, how long do you think you would survive? If you were passing by on horseback and saw a beaten-up man, probably already dead, would you stop to check his pulse, or gallop away as fast as possible?'

We then had something of a lesson in cultural identities. There's nothing in Jesus' story to confirm whether the victim was a Jew or a Samaritan. Jews and Samaritans were identifiable by the way they dressed, but stripped naked, the man who was robbed and left for dead could have been anyone. The Priest and the Levite would have been honour-bound to help a fellow Jew, but because he was unclothed they had every excuse to dismiss him as 'probably a Samaritan'. The Good Samaritan, equally, would have had no idea where the victim came from, but for him, apparently, all that mattered was that he was a fellow human being.

A few birds circled overhead, making real the spectre of a violent and lonely death on the ancient roadway. The desperation and agony of the dying man, the fear that gripped the Priest and the Levite, the risk the Samaritan took with his own safety were all brought home to us as we stood there looking around at the sandy hills, slightly dazed from the heat and privately wishing that we weren't ten minutes walk from the shade.

Back in the bus, we travelled south of the Dead Sea through the wilderness of Zin, and for the first time found ourselves in real desert territory: miles of sandy landscape with only scant vegetation and very few signs of inhabited land. Far from any signs of modern habitation, we stopped at the remains of an ancient city that had been carefully and neatly dug and marked out in the sand. Beneath the upper layers with their first-century Roman features were earlier structures, dating far back into the distant past. We spent all morning looking at the different layers, the shapes of the housing and other buildings, the city walls and the gates, and when we had finished taking notes, Joe sent us on an imaginary tour around the town, suggesting that we walked up and down the streets, pacing out the shape and size of the town and its dwellings.

I got back to the edge of the dig where, just outside the foundations of the city gates, there stood a well. Joe sat down beside me and, as we waited for the others to gather, he said it was the perfect place to envisage the story in John's Gospel where Jesus met a woman who had come to draw water at the well in the middle of the day. It was hot enough to make my head swim merely sitting still, so it must have taken stamina to carry out heavy work drawing and carrying water in the midday heat. But then Joe went on to mention that this area of desert south of Jerusalem was also the land that the patriarchs had walked. There are numerous stories in the Old Testament about the nomadic patriarchs herding their animals from one place to another, and of central importance to this was the digging and redigging of wells.

'There's no way of knowing which well is which,' said Joe, 'or exactly where Abraham or Isaac walked. But what we do know is that there are only so many wells in these desert areas. So although there isn't much you can tie the patriarchal stories to, wells, mountains and rivers are among the few things that remain fairly constant in the landscape. This was, as likely as not, a well that Abraham or Isaac dug.'

I was captured by the idea that in a sometimes featureless wilderness, here was one physical spot where a thread reached back through time to connect us to the patriarchs. According to Genesis, Abraham's family had migrated from Ur of the Chaldees to Haran, where they settled in what seems to have been a sizeable cosmopolitan city. The exact locations of Ur and Haran are uncertain, although some argue that Ur was in Babylonia, at modern-day Tell el-Muqayyar, Iran, and Haran some six hundred miles from there. As an adult, with a household of his own, Abraham heard God calling him to discover a land of promise where God would bless him with enough descendants to make a whole new nation. Leaving his parents behind, Abraham and his wife and nephew and their household embarked on a long journey, taking some years, until they arrived in the desert regions surrounding Israel. There he and his descendants continued to live a nomadic life, moving their flocks from place to place, and their stories are full of accounts of their interaction with other tribes and settlements as they negotiated for water and pasture.

Stories as ancient as Abraham's are undoubtedly a mixture of history, fable, myth and rhetoric, told and retold to establish the national religion and political identity of a growing tribe. I had spent two years at Cambridge learning how to pick my way through ancient texts to try to distinguish which parts are historically accurate and to reassemble them in something like chronological order. It seemed to me not unlike the archaeological work we observed on the digs, where tiny fragments of evidence were assessed and assembled like a jigsaw with many of the pieces missing. But the attempt to reconstruct history from the pieces is only one way of approaching the ancients. Another is to take the story at face value and see what still resonates about the human condition. There are dozens of details in the Old Testament that are culturally and historically so far removed from our experience that it's hard to connect to them, yet here and there the narrative of the lives of these individuals often has a ring of truth about it that – like the little buzz of excitement that comes from sitting by Abraham's well or touching the walls of Jericho – gives the sense of being connected to ancient people who were both not like us at all, and yet thoroughly like us in other ways. And within their stories there emerge different ways of thinking about pilgrimages and faith journeys.

Only in a diary or letters do you get the sense of a story genuinely unfolding stage by stage. Abraham's life story was one long nomadic journey, but like any tale told retrospectively, it's affected by the fact that the narrator knows the end of the story from the beginning. Abraham's call reads as if he heard crystal-clear instructions from God, whereas subsequent moments in his life suggest that he wasn't entirely clear whether he had heard correctly, or even whether he'd imagined the whole thing. Given that God seems to have repeated and even improved on his promises, it's reasonable to suppose that Abraham's sense of calling was – as much as that of a modern-day saint – a hunch he followed with conviction rather than an unmistakable voice. It seemed comforting to me, sitting in the desert and uncertain of my own faith, that perhaps the patriarchs didn't have clarion calls any more than we do.

Abraham's entire story, though, suggests that life itself is a journey towards an ultimate destiny. The promise he staked his life on was of a land to live in, and a large family to inherit it. For Abraham, the meaning of the journey was absolutely dependent upon reaching the destination.

Abraham's grandson, Jacob, later made a journey of his own through the desert, for somewhat ignoble reasons. The third of the great patriarchs in a deeply dysfunctional family, Jacob was the younger of two brothers and was the clear favourite of his mother Rachel, who helped him to trick first his older brother and then his father so that Jacob gained by stealth the inheritance due to the firstborn son. It didn't bring him the ease and wealth he thought it would, for as a result the family was hopelessly divided and Esau, the elder brother, was mad enough to kill Jacob if he could get his hands on him. So Rachel once again tricked the old man and Jacob was sent away, ostensibly to find a wife from among his mother's relatives, but really to escape the fury of his brother.

From these unpromising beginnings Jacob, greedy, dishonest, untrustworthy and on the run, hoped to reinvent himself far from home. Halfway across the desert he lay down to sleep using a stone as a pillow, and in his dreams saw angels walking up and down a ladder that stretched from his makeshift bed to heaven itself. While this might be a blissful dream for someone with a clear conscience, the last thing you would want if you were on the run after your own treachery would be to meet face to face with a God who was supposed to be the epitome of truth and goodness, the judge of humanity. Jacob woke up in a panic, his conscience in overdrive, and proceeded to set up the stone he had slept on as a pillar in honour of God, pouring oil over it while making grand promises about how good he would be from now on. It almost reads as if Jacob was hoping that if he acted with enough religious respect, he could persuade God to overlook his misdemeanours.

> When Jacob awoke from his sleep, he thought, 'Surely
> the LORD is in this place, and I was not aware of it.' He
> was afraid and said, 'How awesome is this place! This is
> none other than the house of God; this is the gateway to
> heaven' . . . He called that place Bethel, though the city
> used to be called Luz. (Genesis 28:16–19)

A convoluted myth evolved concerning Jacob's pillar. The
story runs that it survived through many generations of the
kings of Israel until, after Jerusalem was destroyed in the sixth
century BC, it was brought to Ireland by Jeremiah the prophet.
Later, according to the myth, Columba became the protector
of the pillar in Iona, by which time it was know as the Lia Fail
stone, and this supposedly became the stone upon which
British monarchs were enthroned. This fabulous story is so
lacking in any kind of evidence that it can cheerfully be placed
in the category of historical fiction. But although it's no easy
task to isolate accurate historical detail from Genesis, it became
abundantly clear to us as we traipsed through the deserts of
southern Israel that the stories are based on history. The story
of Jacob's pillar is only one among many Old Testament
accounts of people setting up stones in the desert as altars or
commemorative markers, and the remains of various altars
and small temples are still there to be seen, some within settlements, others seemingly in the middle of nowhere. Like other
ancient civilisations, places where significant things happened
to the patriarchs inspired the need to mark and commemorate them in some way. The big idea in the story of Jacob's
dream, then, is a pilgrimage to a sacred place. He took his

encounter as a sign that this was a holy place where God was especially accessible, and he marked the place as a ritual of worship, and perhaps also so that he could find it again later.

Alongside the idea of sacred space, though, another kind of pilgrimage is evident in the Old Testament. After the patriarchs, Moses the lawgiver also wandered around the desert a good deal, but his journey reflects a more mobile concept of God's presence, symbolised by a tabernacle – a tent-temple which the people took with them wherever they went. Although they were marking out a temporary holy space, the underlying idea was that God's presence travelled with the people, rather than being locked into one geographical spot. The narrative of Moses' life suggests that the journey has meaning in itself: the destination is of secondary importance, while what really matters is the process of transformation that occurs in transit.

Although we didn't meet any pilgrims during our week in the desert, I found that my thoughts about the ancient nomads who had walked there were shaped by the idea of pilgrimage. Their stories all revolve around journeys they made as they followed God's call, but they understood quite differently the significance of their travels and the places they passed through. Abraham travelled with his eyes constantly on his destiny, the meaning of his journey measured by his progress towards the end point. Jacob's trip through the desert was made out of necessity rather than call, but having encountered God's presence unexpectedly he marked the place with a shrine in the belief that in this place God would always be accessible. Moses set off through the desert with a destination in mind, yet in the end it was the journey itself that mattered, for even though he never entered the Promised Land, his life was fulfilled because of the way his wanderings transformed him.

Having recognised prototypes of pilgrimage in the desert, I headed for the library in Jerusalem to look more closely at my idea. I began to discover that there is just as much breadth and variety in the Christian idea of pilgrimage as appeared in the stories of the ancients. To the modern mind, the word 'pilgrimage' summons up more than anything the image of a physical journey with a spiritual purpose: a lengthy walk to a sacred place where some kind of concentrated spiritual power could be found, where prayers might be answered, blessings gained or wisdom sought. But the first few generations of Christians didn't involve themselves in pilgrimages to sacred sites, and largely rejected the idea that God's presence could be tied to particular times or places. Just as Abraham's journey some eighteen hundred years earlier had been a matter of making progress towards a destination where God's promises would be fulfilled, so the early Christians treated all of life as a journey towards heaven as their true destination. From the late second century, however, a steady stream of Christians began to withdraw from society and go to the desert, where they either lived lives of solitary contemplation, or formed small groups that became the precursor to the later monastic communities. More like Moses' sojourn in the desert, their pilgrimage was an inner, spiritual journey for the transformation of the soul.

But when Helena went to find the cross, and the place of

Jesus' death and resurrection, she was grafting into Christian practice a quite different concept of pilgrimage that came from her Greco-Roman background. The Greeks had long treated places of outstanding natural beauty or with unusual geographical features as pagan sacred spaces, and it was common to travel long distances to visit them. Some went alone to plead their cause with the god they believed would be best able to fulfil their needs, but sometimes large contingents would be sent to a sacred shrine to represent the needs of an entire city. These travellers would take offerings to accompany their requests, and some slept beside the shrines in the hopes of being healed. Later they might return with votive offerings – flowers, food or other gifts – to give thanks for answers to their prayers. The gods were also honoured with huge festivals of music and dancing or athletic competitions, the most famous being the shrine to Zeus at Olympia. People travelled from far and wide to attend these great social events, and in the case of the Olympics, the bigger the festival became, the more Zeus' shrine was extended and improved to suit the popularity of the event. Roman culture retained the association of shrines and temples and special places with the presence of their gods, so for Helena it was the most natural thing in the world to treat the geography of the Gospel stories as significant, and the shrines she built were entirely in keeping with the cultural and religious habits with which she had grown up. Helena also went further afield and identified the spot at the foot of Mount Sinai (also called Mount Horeb in the Bible) where, according to tradition, Moses saw a bush that was apparently alight and yet not burning up. The small chapel she built there was later incorporated into St Catherine's Monastery.

Choosing specific places for worship is clearly not unique to the Greco-Roman culture, as evidenced by the impressive stones and the more recently discovered wooden henges at Stonehenge, the hundreds of standing stones around Carnac in northern France, and similar smaller sites all over England and northern Europe that are thought to have been erected for pre-Christian worship. But even apart from religious practices, there seems to be a human instinct to put a marker in the ground at places that mean something to us – either to prove we've been there, or so that we will be able to find our way back there again later. Climb any mountain or high hill in Scotland, Wales or the north of England, and not only at the summit but at various points along the way you'll find a cairn – a pile of stones made by each climber adding their own stone as they pass. Cairns (whose name derive from Gaelic, meaning a pile of stones) seem to have a variety of purposes: astronomical markers, route markings above the treeline for other climbers to follow, burial sites, or simply marks of admiration for the height or outstanding beauty of a particular place. A cairn is a place to sit for a while to rest and enjoy the view, and adding your stone not only gives you a way of marking your own achievement in making it up the hill, it also gives you a sense of connection to others who have stopped there before you. Even the usual British reserve is broken down at cairns: complete strangers talk to each other and swap notes on their climbing experience.

After Helena's building work in Jerusalem, Christian

pilgrimage gradually gathered momentum. The Holy City remained the destination of choice, closely followed by Rome, but gradually a host of other cities were added to the pilgrim's wish list. When Chaucer introduced the Wife of Bath as a well-travelled pilgrim, he noted that she had already visited five of the six great medieval pilgrimage sites: Jerusalem, Rome, Boulogne, Cologne and Santiago. Canterbury completed the list. But what distinguished these six places?

Jerusalem was, of course, the birthplace of Christianity, and therefore the most important destination. But Rome quickly rose in importance. When Christianity first found its way there in the first century, it was unrecognised as a religion by the Roman Empire, its followers were persecuted and it was perceived as the faith of the poor and dispossessed. By the early fourth century it had not only survived but established itself as an unofficial religion. Persecution ceased when Constantine made it legal in AD 313. Sixty-seven years later, Emperor Theodosius declared Christianity the official religion of the Roman Empire, and thus it was that as the empire declined, Christianity replaced the dying Roman religions.

Among those martyred at Rome were two of the most recognised Christian saints of the first century – St Peter and St Paul – and in AD 330 Constantine ordered the construction of St Peter's Basilica over the oratory of St Peter's tomb on Vatican Hill, where Peter had been crucified upside down. Rome immediately became a pilgrimage site for Christians who, grateful for the longed-for freedom to practise their faith without fear of persecution, travelled to pray at the tombs of St Peter and St Paul (whose tomb was later covered with the Basilica of St Paul Outside The Walls). The Bishop of Rome, on account of being the successor to St Peter, was thereafter regarded as having primacy over all other Western bishops and was exempt from imperial authority.

In the fourteenth century conflict over the role of the papacy in secular leadership led to a temporary relocation to Avignon from 1309 to 1378, through the rule of seven popes, but even then Rome continued to flourish as a Holy City, and remained second only to Jerusalem in popularity as a pilgrim site. Over time many other churches, religious buildings, museums and libraries were added, and countless major works of art. Many thousands of pilgrims still make their way to Rome each year. For devout Catholics a highlight would be catching a glimpse of the pope as he emerges onto the balcony above St Peter's Square to pronounce a blessing, but for Christians of all denominations Rome is packed with attractions, including the stairs of St Peter that a true pilgrim climbs on his or her knees as an act of penance, and the Basilica of St Mary Major which contains a reliquary said to contain pieces of wood from the manger in which Jesus was laid as a baby.

Boulogne's present-day cathedral was built in the nine-teenth-century Catholic revival because, like many other churches in France, the old cathedral had been destroyed in the Revolution. The original cathedral, though, was built to celebrate the legend of Notre Dame. The story goes that in about 633, when St Omer was Bishop of Boulogne, a mysterious boat with no oars, no sails and no sailors on board sailed into the estuary of the River Liane at Boulogne carrying a luminous statue of the Virgin Mary. The local residents carried the statue up to their church, and soon miracles began to be attributed to the presence of the Virgin. Another version of the story has it that the mysterious boat was pulled along by a swan, which then became the emblem of the town. Pilgrimages to Boulogne became immensely popular in the medieval era, and people would travel from far and wide to kneel before the statue. This in turn was of economic benefit to Boulogne – inns and lodging houses flourished with the pilgrim trade, the local craftspeople sold small trinkets made from lead, and the giving of alms and donations made the monastery attached to the cathedral a prosperous community.

Cologne was the final resting place of the Magi or 'three kings' of the Christmas story. Their relics were kept in Constantinople until 344, then given to Milan by Bishop Eustorgius. There they remained until 1164, when the Holy Roman Emperor Frederick Barbarossa gave them to Rainauld of Dassel, Archbishop of Cologne, and from that day on Cologne became a pilgrim destination. A shrine in the shape of a sarcophagus was built for the relics, renowned medieval goldsmith Nicholas of Verdun being among the craftsmen who worked on it, and once the shrine was complete in about 1225, plans were laid to build a cathedral to house the shrine. The cathedral was built over six centuries, and is to this day Europe's largest Gothic ecclesiastical structure. The significance of the Magi to the history of Cologne is reflected in the three golden crowns on the city's coat of arms.

Santiago de Compostela in northern Spain is supposedly the burial place of St James, the brother of St John. James and John were two of Jesus' favourite disciples, and he nicknamed them the Sons of Thunder. According to legend, James had brought Christianity to Spain and subsequently returned to Judea. After his death, through a series of miracles, his body was returned to Spain and the church and the city of Santiago were gradually erected around him. In medieval times the various routes through northern Spain to Santiago were inhospitable and this was considered the most difficult pilgrimage of all.

Of all the shrines in England, the most popular was Thomas à Becket's in Canterbury, where pilgrims came to seek healing for illnesses.

> And specially from every shire's end
> Of England they to Canterbury wend,
> The holy blessed martyr there to seek
> Who helped them when they lay so ill and weak.[3]

Becket had been murdered on 29 December 1170, and the anniversary of his death was kept every year until he was made a saint in 1220 and his feast day was transferred to 7 July, probably because – as Chaucer pointed out in the General Prologue to *The Canterbury Tales* – pilgrimages were usually made in the spring and early summer when people got the urge for a change of scene after a long winter, and the weather conditions made travel easier (it's thought, for instance, that Watling Street, originally the Roman road from London to

Canterbury, may have been largely impassable in the winter, especially in the valleys). The fact that people came 'from every shire's end / Of England' is reflected in the large number of ancient tracks that radiate out from Canterbury.

A pilgrimage in medieval times, whether on foot or horseback, was often a tough enterprise to begin with, and some routes were fraught with danger, poor food and inadequate accommodation, which sometimes led to illness or even death. The relics of saints found at such places were, as often as not, unlikely to be genuine, and the stories associated with them the stuff of fairy tales. Yet now, as then, this seems not to diminish the powerful effect they have on the pilgrim. A 'willing suspension of disbelief', as Coleridge would have put it, is part of the pilgrimage experience: the power of the ritual lies not in the proof of the evidence, but in the effect it has on those who take part in it. The tradition of pilgrimage is built not around the historical authenticity either of the legends or the relics, but around the tradition they encapsulate, and the investment in that tradition over hundreds of years by countless pilgrims and visitors in itself adds layers of meaning to a particular place.

By the late medieval era an important element of pilgrimage was *curiositas* – a desire to travel, and to see and understand the world that lay beyond one's own experience, and perhaps to bring home some souvenirs and reminders of what had been learned. This aspect of pilgrimage was often criticised as being detrimental to spiritual pursuits, but it became apparent – although the Reformation eventually put an end to the practice of pilgrimage – that the thirst for adventure and knowledge would not recede. *Curiositas* kept alive the desire to travel, and the wealthy and aristocratic continued to visit traditional pilgrimage sites and to explore further afield. By the eighteenth century the Grand Tour had developed, and pilgrimage had given way to a fully fledged cultural and educational tourism.

Interest in travel to the Holy Land revived in the nineteenth century, after discoveries in Egypt and throughout the Middle East opened up interest in the history of the area. Wealthy individuals made trips to Palestine, and in the last three decades of the nineteenth century Thomas Cook, famed for developing tourism, began his work with a spiritual motivation, taking twelve thousand people to tour Palestine and introducing them to the history and devotional aspects of Christianity.

The late nineteenth and early twentieth centuries saw a new interest in British pilgrimage sites. British cathedrals became desirable places to visit, not merely to attend Divine Service, but to absorb the combination of history, culture and spirituality offered there. Throughout the twentieth century other medieval pilgrimage sites such as Canterbury and Walsingham underwent revivals, and as interest grew in 'Celtic' Christianity, Iona was once again visited by large numbers and Lindisfarne began to draw pilgrims. Catholic Marian shrines such as Lourdes and Fatima continued to draw the crowds, and in the latter half of the twentieth century Protestant attitudes concerning pilgrimage relaxed and Christians of all denominations engaged in pilgrimage. Taizé, an ecumenical monastery, was begun in France by

Brother Roger as a means of healing the spiritual wounds of Europe through two world wars, and thousands of people of all ages – but especially young adults – travelled from all over the world to spend some time living in the Taizé rhythm of life.

Interestingly, then, the revival of pilgrimage was in part inspired by the very reasons why I was in Jerusalem myself – interest in the history of places whose significance had begun as devotional. Instead of regarding my studious approach to the place as somehow prior in significance, I began to realise that without the centuries of pilgrims keeping interest in such places alive, there would probably be no studies of the kind I was making. How easy it is to assume, in the throes of the latest and most modern study techniques, that our fore-bears were ignorant and unenlightened. The humbling truth remains that from one generation to another, even in our greatest achievements, we stand on the shoulders of giants.

Back in Jerusalem for our final week, we retraced some of our steps to visit again some of the most remarkable sights we had seen, and one or two places we had missed in the first week. Last, but not least, we walked to Bethlehem to see the traditional birthplace of Christ.

I already knew that, as told in school nativity plays, the story is a mixture of history and fable, and that many of the details have been overlaid with the culture of northern Europe. There's no dispute that Jesus lived, and was a renowned religious leader. But the date of his birth might have been several years BC or AD, wasn't in December, wasn't in a garden shed with holly and robins and snow, and could

43

just as easily have been in Nazareth as Bethlehem. So when we arrived in Bethlehem Square after a long walk along a hot and dusty road, I was somewhat lacking in awe and anticipation, and was more concerned with making sure we got a break and a long drink before embarking on another round of picking through layers of history.

Joe called us together in the square and told us we would look first at the church built over the birthplace, and then go down into the cave that is supposed to be Jesus' birthplace. The artisan houses we had seen in the slopes of the ancient wall of David's city were all built around a central room where the family animals were kept, not only for security, but also because they kept the house warm at night. But a few miles further south, Bethlehem is built on rocky ground, and beneath the road level is a system of caves. It seems that these natural shelters – which, far from being freezing outhouses, have a steady, warm, year-round temperature – were used to house animals beneath Bethlehem's homes.

'You are all well aware by now,' said Joe, 'that the stable Jesus was born in wasn't a wooden garden shed. But, if he was born in Bethlehem, it was either in this cave or in one pretty close to this spot. Bethlehem isn't that big; there aren't all that many caves to choose from!'

The cave itselt is quite small, with a door to either side through which visitors enter and exit, and the focal point is a decorative star in the floor that marks the place where the manger stood. I stood looking at the stream of people praying, crossing themselves, singing, kneeling to kiss the star, all the while considering the possibility that Jesus had really been born some seventy miles to the north, in Nazareth. But I decided to wait there in the little cave until there was a gap in the traffic so that I could take a photo. After ten minutes or so my opportunity came. The last of about seventy people disappeared through the exit, and for just a few minutes no one else entered. I was ready, camera in hand, to capture the moment. But then, unexpectedly, it was as if some other, numinous presence suddenly filled the room. No angels, no voices, nothing tangible that I could identify. Just a great, timeless sense of eternity, and instead of the great puzzle of divine existence, the air seemed heavy with a profoundly loving presence. Slipping my camera back into my pocket, I knelt down before the star and gave in to the sense of wonder. Minutes later the next wave of human traffic began to flow in, and the moment passed.

As we entered the final few days of our tour, I thought about the difference between a student, a tourist and a pilgrim. I had set out on this trip clear that I was not going to involve myself in strange, anti-intellectual practices, and I was determined to make sure I didn't waste any time on ancient superstitions and relics that had nothing to do with reality. Yet among the many things I learned about the land and its history, I also learned that it isn't so easy to separate theory and practice, that pilgrimage was the precursor to the very journey I was making, and that my concept of what was 'real' was too much wrapped up in a very modern view of history.

Theology, according to several of the major Protestant denominations, equally appeals to Scripture, reason and tradition (some would also add experience). A child of my time, I was obsessed with reason, and had failed to understand that tradition is inescapably part of being human.

You can't judge by appearance, of course, and I will never know whether the handbag-waving pilgrims I'd encountered on the Mount of Olives had been transformed by their experience or not. But they had formed part of my impression that calling yourself a pilgrim doesn't necessarily make you any more than a tourist, while insisting that you are a student doesn't stop you, accidentally, from becoming a pilgrim after all.

In the libraries of Cambridge I had discovered that mining the biblical text in the original languages unlocks many of the mysteries of the Old and New Testaments. Here in the sun-drenched desert, the land itself began to give up some of its secrets, as standing on one dig or ruin after another, the remains of Bronze Age city walls or second-century Christian communities began to frame the complex jigsaw of ancient history into something that made sense. As I began to see more clearly how the story of Christianity had emerged out of its Jewish heritage, I also gained clearer mental images of the poetry of the Psalms, and the parables Jesus told, and the narratives of the Gospel writers. The cattle on a thousand hills, the rose of Sharon, the cedars of Lebanon, the wilderness and the cleft in the rock all began to lose their soft, lush Englishness in my imagination, and take on a sharper focus. 'God makes my feet like the feet of a gazelle,' wrote Habakkuk the prophet, 'he makes me able to go on the heights' – a description that had always seemed to put spiritual greatness as far out of reach for me as the elegance and gracefulness of a ballet dancer. But the small mountain gazelles on these hillsides were not tall and elegant at all, but compact little creatures that bounded about with unpredictable, vertical jumps reminiscent of a hare. Their comical, childlike movements seemed to bring into the realm of possibility the invitation to walk a spiritual path as envisaged by the ancient mystics.

Nothing had really changed in my discomfort with dark, smoky old churches, nor in my suspicion of the kind of religion that expects you to leave your brain at the door. Yet despite myself, I realised that the Holy Land had begun to work its magic on me. Walking through streets where Jesus had walked, deserts Abraham had crossed and up mountains Moses and Elijah had climbed, I hadn't lost my ability to separate fact from fiction, but the experience had, nonetheless, shifted my perspective on what was important in life. The climate had taught me that you have to adapt yourself to the circumstances, not only on a summer trip, but in the journey of life. The colossal figures of the Old Testament may have been passed down to us in part-myth, part-history, but despite this I had learned from them that there are different ways to approach God, different motivations to adopt in searching for the divine, different ways of working out what it means to be human and spiritual in contrary motion to the assumptions of the time. I had realised that there were things in my approach to life that I could change if I wanted to, and some things about the world that were beyond my ability to do anything about. I was more certain about some things, and less certain about others.

It might only be visible in minute, incremental steps, but I knew that something had shifted inwardly, so that as I began packing my bags I knew I was returning to England with less rigid boundaries between history and tradition, story and doctrine. I was returning home feeling less secure, but more whole. I hadn't set out on a pilgrimage, and yet by the end of the trip I had found myself drawn into something more profound than a study trip – I'd become, in a way, an accidental pilgrim. The difference between a tourist and a pilgrim is that, while a tourist travels to get away from it all before going back to reality, a pilgrim is transformed by the experience and returns home changed. Dee Dyas wrote that for the pilgrim, 'the observer becomes a participant, and the experience of travel becomes infused with recognition of the need for change, whether this signifies healing for mind or body, inner peace, or a new perspective on life'.[4]

The day before we were due to fly home to England, I called my lecturer, who had just arrived in Israel. True to his word, he took me to have tea in a beautiful old café in the Muslim Quarter.

'So how has the trip been?' he asked.

'It's been great,' I said, 'but not really what I expected. The history has been fantastic, the tour group were a mixed bag, and the pilgrims we kept meeting were quite annoying at times. I got spat at, I got sunstroke, I began to completely disbelieve some of my own religious assumptions, and there were days when I felt completely disconnected from people who wanted to keep stopping to pray. But you were right about the place getting under your skin. It's not that I had a big religious experience, more as if just a few things have deepened and a lot of other things that I thought mattered suddenly don't seem important any more.'

He thought for a minute and sipped his tea. Then he said, 'The longer I live, the fewer things I believe in, but I believe them more deeply than ever before. I was brought up with a great many doctrines, and thought they all mattered. But now – I believe only three things. I believe God is there, I believe that God is love, and I believe Jesus is God's Son, whatever that means, exactly. Everything else is pretty much up for debate.'

I took a breath, and almost began to tell him about the moment in the cave at Bethlehem, and then thought better of it. I closed my mouth again. I needed to process that a while longer in my own head before I told anyone else.

He smiled. 'I'm not going to say *I told you so*. But I think you've caught the bug, Maggi, and I think the end of this trip might be just the beginning of something for you. *L' shanah haba'ah b'Yerushalayim.* Next year, in Jerusalem.'

2

Pushchair pilgrim

Shall I take my tiny boat across the wide sparkling ocean?
Ascribed to St Brendan the Navigator before sailing
across the Atlantic

The trip to Israel had undone all my preconceptions of pilgrimage: old images of dark and dreary churches, old bones, superstitious rituals and excessively worthy people in terrible clothes had been replaced by the idea of journeys into spiritual transformation. It felt as though my mental antennae had been retuned, and everywhere I looked there seemed to be someone going on a pilgrimage, returning from one, or urging me to read books about them. I was longing to plan the next big trip right away, but I knew I needed to settle down to study for my finals. Just before term began, though, I was in Durham for a short conference, and with two days to spare before returning south I decided to go a little further north to Holy Island.

I wasn't a complete stranger to Lindisfarne, having been there once before, but all I remembered was the beach, the castle and the anxious reading of tide timetables to ensure I wasn't cut off from the mainland. This time I wanted to travel thoughtfully, and consider at length what it might mean to be a present-day pilgrim. With a mix of hope and curiosity I wondered whether I might discover what people meant when they spoke of 'thin places' where earth seems to touch heaven.

There's a Celtic saying that earth and heaven are only three feet apart, but in thin places the distance between them narrows; the veil between earth and heaven becomes almost imperceptible, and you can catch a glimpse of the glory of God. It's as if a door between heaven and earth is not quite closed, and through the crack in the door the bright light of eternity shines. Thin places are nearly always wild landscapes, and often close to the seashore, which in itself suggests a liminal space, a literal line drawn in the sand at the edge of the world. Rugged coastlines are redolent of the unpredictability of nature, and draw out our awareness that life is, ultimately, beyond our control.

These are the obvious reasons why such landscapes became known as thin places, but in addition to their wild beauty the awareness that generations of others have made their own spiritual discoveries there affirms such places as having this quality and builds a sense of expectation. Here spiritual knowledge extends beyond what can be learned in a chapel or library; the untamed landscape seems to draw the pilgrim, body and soul, into the immediacy of the experience of faith. An anonymous ninth-century Welsh poet wrote, 'Almighty Creator, it is you who have made the land and the sea . . . It is difficult to express its measure. Letters cannot contain it, letters cannot contain it.'[1]

Some of Lindisfarne's mystique lies in its semi-isolation from the mainland. Access is via a tidal causeway, or by walking the nearby and much older pilgrims' route, marked by stakes or staves that stick up from the sand all the way from the mainland to the island and described by Sir Walter Scott in his narrative poem *Marmion*:

> Dry shod, o'er sands, twice every day,
> The pilgrims to the shrine find way;
> Twice every day, the waves efface
> Of staves and sandalled feet the trace.[2]

Scott was writing of Lindisfarne as he imagined it in 1513, with the abbey still standing, and it's a poem well worth reading (even though it's a grim tale) and includes a description of the abbess and five nuns travelling there from Whitby Abbey by sea. Late medieval pilgrims often travelled in groups, and took the sea route to avoid the dangers they might encounter in the woods – such as poor roads, outlaws or wild animals such as wolves and wild boar – so Scott's nuns arrived on the far side of the island rather than walking the pilgrims' route.

Arriving from the mainland, though, you can still follow the staves across the sand, or walk or drive along the more recently built causeway, during the hours when the tide is low. The island feels fairly remote even with a good number of day-trippers present, but once they have left a deep peace and stillness envelops the island.

The small town is easily in view once you reach the island, and a little further on are the ruins of the Norman abbey. This was built over the original Anglo-Saxon monastery, founded in AD 635 by Aidan, a Scots-Celtic monk from Iona and first Bishop of Lindisfarne, who prayed for the island with these words:

> Lord, this bare island,
> make it a place of peace.
> Here be the peace
> of those who do Thy will.
> Here be the peace
> of brother serving man.
> Here be the peace
> of holy monks obeying.
> Here be the peace
> of praise by dark and day.
> Be this Island Thy Holy Island.
> I, Lord, Thy servant, Aidan,
> make this prayer.
> Be it Thy care.
> Amen.[3]

It's thought that Aidan chose the island because, while it was suitably remote for a monastic community, it was also reasonably close to Bamburgh, the capital of Northumbria, which lies on the coast just south of the island. This was the seat of King Oswald, who was much in favour of Aidan spreading the message of Christianity and sometimes travelled with him to act as his interpreter.

When Aidan died in AD 651, a teenage shepherd boy called Cuthbert witnessed the moment of his death in a vision, after which he too felt the call to the monastic life. After three years in a monastery at Tweeddale in the Scottish Borders, he moved to Lindisfarne where he was first monk, then abbot and later Bishop of Lindisfarne. Cuthbert was reputed to be a healer and miracle worker, and during his life visitors came to the island to ask for his prayers. But he was confirmed as a saint when, eleven years after his death in 687, his body was discovered to be incorrupt. The significance given to sainthood at that time is illustrated by the fact that far more pilgrims flocked to the island after his death than during his life.

Today there is plenty to see in the village, which is home to less than two hundred people. St Mary's Church stands on the edge of the community and there are a number of pilgrim houses in the streets nearby, as well as small cafés and hostelries where sweet Lindisfarne mead can be sampled. The extensive abbey ruins are well enough preserved to get an idea of the size and lifestyle of the community when it was at its height. Between the church and the abbey ruins stands a tall, elegant statue of Aidan, bringing the early saints constantly to mind. But the best experience to be had on Lindisfarne is to walk away from the town and the ruins and – as the early community of monks did – to enjoy the kind of isolation that is rarely found in our densely populated islands.

There were plenty of moments in history when God's name was used as an excuse for unilateral action, both in a political context to justify conquests, and by Church hierarchies who imposed forms of worship and church order on local communities, sometimes through a well-intentioned desire to maintain unity, but sometimes, it seems, through an unholy struggle for power. This is, perhaps, one reason why the early Celtic monastic communities seem to us now to represent a gentler and more noble form of mission – for despite the fact that, being of their time, their communities were more authoritarian than we would find comfortable, they did deliberately grow their own localised form of Christianity, rather than imposing a cultural format from elsewhere. There is, in reality, very little evidence available to us as to the practices of early Celtic Christianity, and what now passed under the title is nine parts modern invention. But that doesn't necessarily make it bad in itself: what's most interesting about this recent trend is, perhaps, its renewed intent to find a way of living out the Christian faith that makes sense in its own time and culture. What is so appealing to the modern mind about the early Celtic communities, I think, is that they allowed the local community some licence to shape their own pattern of life and worship.

For me, still processing my thoughts about Israel, this trip was an opportunity to think about how that impulse affected me. Faith has to feel as though it fits the person who professes it – and for me that meant holding faith as a woman, a musician and someone for whom intellectual credibility is a high priority. But at the same time faith is not a purely individualistic concern; it is only in the last century or so that individualism has been allowed to shape faith to any great degree, and for faith to be authentic it also needs to remain congruent with its more universal expressions, both historically and geographically. In those days on Lindisfarne, I wanted to consider the balance between these things as they applied to me: given that I often felt that the traditional, institutional forms of faith felt alien to me, how was I to fit myself into the Church in a way that respected the foundational truths of the gospel while still allowing me to be 'myself'?

There is a difference between the kind of navel-gazing that is an exercise in individualism, and the kind of self-knowledge required for fitting oneself into the world. Michel de Montaigne expressed the fine balance between these two things, suggesting that for a person to be properly in control of herself the first thing she needs to do is to cede control: the kind of attitude that makes people demanding and bossy and unable to fit in with others. There is a sense in which understanding your true self and feeling at home in your own skin is not a selfishly driven quest, but the key to finding your place in the world. At the end of his *Essays*, Montaigne writes:

> It is an absolute perfection and virtually divine to know how to enjoy our being rightfully. We seek other conditions because we do not understand the use of our own . . . Yet there is no use our mounting on stilts, for on stilts we must still walk on our own legs. And on the loftiest throne in the world we are still sitting only on our own behind.[4]

It doesn't take long to walk across Holy Island, but once on the other side there are few signs of civilisation – a few sheep here and there, and some boats out at sea are all that invade the landscape. Sitting on the beach without a soul in sight, looking out at the North Sea as the tide began to come in, I had the chance to think without any distractions, and to consider how I might 'enjoy my being rightfully'. It's hard to say what I expected of a 'thin place' – what it might mean, exactly, to come close to heaven. I can't say I had any kind of out-of-this-world revelation, or that I felt God was more present there, or that my particular mixture of faith and doubt was particularly well resolved. But far away from the distractions of the world, aware that somewhere behind me the mainland was gradually being cut off, it did seem easier to think clearly and to gain some sense of perspective on life. It reminded me in some ways of the kind of feeling you get travelling by air – far above the world, things that normally seem overwhelming and all-consuming suddenly seem cut right down to size. And here, cut off by the tide, small squabbles of church order and theological correctness were reduced to their proper place. My own sense of place in the world was restored: not too important, yet not insignificant either. The ever-expanding universe of my own life seemed to find its centre again, and that, it seemed to me, was the way in which this faraway place created a sense of touching another dimension.

Some of the idea of the thin space, I think, comes from the mixture of beauty and isolation, and the long tradition of others finding this to be a place of increased perception. But on these northern islands, perhaps it also has to do with being not just on the coast, but quite surrounded by the sea. Living in the British Isles, the sea is never far away, and some of my biggest life decisions have been made at the seashore. It seems to me to be a liminal space: it quite literally draws a line in the sand at the edge of the world and the boundary of the mysterious deeps.

The dark and disturbing mystery of the ocean and its power to swallow people alive is reason enough to fear and respect the sea, which no doubt was why ancient Jewish and Christian theology saw it as symbolic of chaos and darkness, adding a few mythical sea monsters into the mix to reinforce its uncontrollable mystery. As it turned out, it was precisely from the dark horizon of the North Sea that the events of the ninth century tore apart the peace and tranquillity of the early Lindisfarne community. The *Anglo-Saxon Chronicle* reported that in AD 793 the Viking raids began on Northumbria, 'which sorely affrighted the inhabitants . . . A great famine followed hard on these signs, and a little later in that same year, on the 8th of June, the harrying of the heathen miserably destroyed God's church by rapine and slaughter.'

It was perhaps a tad rich for the Anglo-Saxon chroniclers to paste the caricature of rape and pillage onto the Vikings, given that their ancestors had invaded Britain less than three centuries earlier. But there's no doubt that the Viking raids did deplete both the wealth and the confidence of the Lindisfarne monks over the following decades, and in AD 875 they fled the island, taking Cuthbert's body with them. Cuthbert had wanted to be buried at Lindisfarne, but his dying words had taken into account the turbulent times in which they lived:

> If necessity compels you to choose between one of two evils, I would much rather you take my bones from their

> tomb and carry them away with you to whatever place of
> rest God may decree, rather than consent to iniquity
> and put your necks under the yokes of schismatics.

In St Mary's Church, close to the abbey ruins, stands a large
wooden sculpture of the monks bearing away Cuthbert's body[5]
– which, if it really was incorrupt, must have weighed a good
bit. It's a testament to their attention to his words, and to their
reluctance to be parted from their beloved saint, that they
didn't falter in taking him with them, especially when you
consider that after leaving the island they moved repeatedly
for a hundred and twenty years before eventually settling in
their permanent home at Durham. There Cuthbert's body still
lies in the cathedral, visited to this day by pilgrims. I concluded
my own brief pilgrimage with a visit to his tomb before returning home. All the way south I thought of those monks, restless
and homeless for a hundred and twenty years after leaving the
peace of their beloved island, travelling from one place to
another like pilgrims with no certain destination.

Back in Cambridge my feet hardly touched the ground before
the year was in full swing, intense work for finals being punctu-
ated with several rounds of applications for funding for further
study. I didn't travel the following summer, and I had just begun
my PhD studies when the subject of pilgrimage came up again.
One afternoon in the university library tea rooms, I ran into a
friend whom I'd met playing in a jazz band. He was studying

medieval history, but his real dream was to become a writer, and he spent much of his spare time inventing fantasy stories based on some of the medieval lore he was reading by day. Over a cup of tea he announced happily that he had almost finished his dissertation, and had just landed a book contract to walk from Canterbury to Santiago de Compostela and then write an account of his travels. With months of library isolation stretching ahead of me, I felt a twinge of envy over completed deadlines and a grand adventure to look forward to.

'Just think,' he said brightly, seeming to read my mind, 'while you're buried in the library I'll be doing my research out on the open road!'

I smiled at his bubbling excitement. 'So will you travel light, or take a tent?'

'I'll camp,' said Ben, 'but only when it's strictly necessary. I'll stay wherever I can find a bed. I'll stay in the shelters along the Camino when I get that far. But through France I'm hoping I might blag a space in a barn, or even a bed for the night here and there if I meet interesting locals. And with that in mind, my concession to travelling light is that I'm taking my trombone with me.'

'You *are* joking?' I said, trying to summon up an image of a backpack with a trombone attached.

'No, really, I mean it – partly for the novelty value, I suppose, but otherwise I would miss being able to play for months on end. You never know – I might do a bit of busking, earn a bit of cash, and meet some interesting people.'

A few weeks later Ben set out from Canterbury, and over the following months sent brief news updates whenever he came across an Internet connection. Sure enough, his trombone playing made him friends wherever he went, and he regularly slept in barns or outhouses and woke up to French farmhouse breakfasts. His tales of walking through France and Spain made me realise how different the modern experience of travel is from the medieval pilgrims who – like him – would have made journeys of hundreds of miles on foot or horseback. Planes and high-speed trains make it possible to get to places previously undreamed of, yet what is missed is any tangible concept of the distances travelled or the incremental changes of culture and climate being passed over without so much as a backwards glance. Ben was taking in every footstep of his journey, and his notes every few days rekindled my own interest in making a long pilgrimage. I began to consider the possibility of a three- or four-week trip the following summer, and spent tea breaks doodling ideas of where I might travel. Were I to follow the Wife of Bath's example and complete the whole set of medieval pilgrimages with trips to Cologne, Boulogne, Rome and Santiago, it might take several trips, not just one. But the more I read, the more I discovered intriguing possibilities among the lesser-known shrines, and one that really caught my imagination was Rocamadour, a shrine built halfway up the side of a gorge and accessible only by climbing steep steps from the town below. I put a pin in the map, promised myself I would go there one day, and went back to the north wing of the library where Coleridge awaited my attention.

Two years on, I was more than halfway through my PhD studies at the university, fulfilling various placements and extra pieces of work for my qualifications from theological college, and in conversation with the diocese of the Church of England where I was soon to be ordained. Trying to satisfy three institutions at the same time had its complications, for they all had their sets of rules and guidelines, and when they clashed each of them believed they took priority over the others, leaving me no choice but to pick which one to let down. So I had got fairly used to irate people telling me, 'You can't do that!' But in those first few years in which women were ordained as priests, I had got used to hearing the words 'you can't' repeated too often: 'You can't be on the preaching rota, you can take care of the crèche,' or, 'You can't come to this meeting, it's for men only,' or, 'You can't wear that/say that/do that,' and, should I ever venture to complain, 'You can't expect people to be nice to you, they didn't want a woman priest in the first place.' I convinced myself that if I stayed focused I would be able to withstand this barrage of negativity. 'None of it's meant personally,' I told myself. 'Don't let it get you down.'

Life had undergone a far more profound change in those two years, though, because by this time I was also a mother. I had longed for a baby for many years, only for him to turn up after I had almost given up hope. A few months before he was due, it had emerged that there were no guidelines for an ordinand needing to take maternity leave, and new rules had to be invented to accommodate me. Of course I wasn't going to let the Church's frustration over the inconvenience of a pregnant ordinand dampen my happiness – never was a child more wanted and more welcomed by a mother. But we did have something of a rocky start. The birth was long and complicated and the early months very unsettled and sleepless as I found my way through difficulties that only made sense years later when my son was diagnosed with Asperger's syndrome. It would be extravagant to say we settled into a routine, but we sort of bumbled along. The most peaceful part of each day came in the afternoons when, strapped close to me in a sling, he slept while I made my escape into my books and, in small but steady steps, continued with my PhD thesis. Post-partum hormones, extreme tiredness and Coleridge's complex ideas proved a dizzying combination, and thoughts of pilgrimage were far from my mind when, one evening, the phone rang.

'Do you want to come to France?' said my friend. 'We've booked an enormous house in the Dordogne, and a pile of friends are coming with us. There's loads of room – come and join us!'

What possible reply could there be but 'yes'? A holiday on a budget that I didn't have to plan was like a gift from heaven, so a few months later we pitched up in a small hamlet in south-west France, where the first few days of the holiday disappeared in the exploration of local markets, and hours of reading and chatting over local food and wine while we admired the mountains and sunsets from the large balcony. After supper one evening we got the map out to see what lay further afield. We discussed various beauty spots that would be worth a visit, and a couple of foodie friends had found out where the farmers' markets and vineyards were so we could try out all the local specialities. But as we pored over the map, my eyes fell on a familiar name, some seventy miles to the west.

'Rocamadour!' I cried. 'I didn't realise it was so close. I've wanted to go there for ages.'

'Too far!' said one person. 'We've just driven hundreds of miles to get here!'

'There are better views in the other direction,' said another.

'Stay local for a couple of days,' said our resident food expert. 'The best markets are in the next two days.'

After weighing up the relative attractions in each direction, no one was persuaded by my enthusiasm, but to me it seemed almost magical that without any planning on my part I had landed so close to Rocamadour. So the next morning I packed the car with a map and picnic and the unbelievably large quantity of equipment that parents of small children accumulate, settled my son into his car seat, and set off.

Rocamadour is a small town nestled in the limestone rocks that rise above the River Alzou, a tributary of the Dordogne, in the Commune of Lot in south-west France. The cliffs rise sharply above the town, and just over half way up, on a rocky ledge, stand various chapels and monastery buildings built around a cave where a hermit named Amadour once lived. Right at the top of the cliff is a castle, which was built to protect the shrine against attacks from above.

Long before Christianity came to the region, the cave had been a sacred site of the goddess Cybele, an ancient mother figure who combined the identities of several other goddesses, but by the Middle Ages Rocamadour was a celebrated Marian pilgrimage site. At least as early as the eleventh century there are records of Christian pilgrims travelling to Rocamadour to offer prayers at the shrine of a carved wooden statue of the Madonna, known as the Black Virgin, around whom a small chapel had been built. Then in 1166 an incorrupt body was found buried in a cave next to the chapel, and its identity was taken to be the body of St Amadour.

As to who exactly Amadour was, there are a few theories but none is conclusive. The earliest records of his life appear in the *Acts of St Amadour*, a book that probably dates back to the twelfth century, which claims that Amadour was a first-century saint. Others have suggested that Amadour was an alternative name for St Amator, who was Bishop of Auxerre from 388 to 418, while others believe him simply to have been an unknown hermit. The absence of any clear evidence as to his true identity has, however, allowed a more fabulous myth to persist, which is that Zacchaeus, the tax collector who shinned up a sycamore tree to get a good view of Jesus (Luke 19:1–10), later fled his homeland when Christians came under persecution, and together with his wife, St Veronica, boarded a small boat and was guided by angels to the coast of Aquitaine where Zacchaeus adopted the French name Amadour. From there they travelled to Rome, and later returned again to France, and after Veronica's death Amadour withdrew to the hills. Guided once again by angels, he found Cybele's cave shrine, and there he remained as a hermit until his death around AD 70. This version of the

legend claims that he installed into this cave the wooden
statue of the Black Virgin, which some say was carved by St
Luke, while others claim that Zacchaeus carved it himself.

So much for the legends. Scientific analysis suggests that
the Black Virgin, carved out of walnut wood, actually dates
from the ninth or tenth centuries. At that time, pilgrims
walking through France en route to Santiago passed along
the top of the cliff, often stopping at a shelter in L'Hospitalet,
a nearby hamlet. Most bypassed the shrine at Rocamadour,
but as it was believed the Black Virgin would bring fertility to
brides, a few made the descent down the cliff face to pray for
their wives or other female relatives. By the late twelfth
century, though, once Rocamadour had a saint as well as a
statue, and reports began to abound of miraculous healings
and conversions, pilgrims began to flock to the cave.

The fortunes of Rocamadour rose and fell as pilgrimage
declined through the Reformation. The Church of Notre
Dame, built around the original shrine in 1479, was pillaged
by Protestant iconoclasts in 1562 and damaged by fire, and St
Amadour's body was destroyed. But the Black Virgin
remained unharmed, and in the 1880s reconstruction of the
church began. To this day the town is one of the most-visited
tourist sites in France, and the shrine is among the most
popular Marian pilgrim sites.

This odd mix of natural beauty and Greek and Christian
legend was the place I was now approaching, not on foot or
horseback, but in a nippy little French car full of baby equipment. Although I was pretty certain it would be difficult to
climb up to the shrine with a toddler in tow, the guidebook

said there was an elevator. But on arrival at Rocamadour I found that it was closed for repairs. My heart sank as my hopes of seeing the shrine dwindled away, for to get to the shrine from the town you have to climb 216 steps up the steep cliff to the plateau. I could see some pilgrims already making the ascent painfully on their knees, in the traditional manner of penance. There was no way I could make a pilgrimage up steep steps in the side of a mountain with a toddler in a push-chair. We were so tantalisingly near, and yet so disappointingly far from seeing the chapels and the Black Virgin. What had I been thinking? 'You can't . . .' The familiar voice sounded inside my head, and behind it echoed the chorus of voices from home: you can't be a priest, you're a woman; you can't do a PhD and have a baby; you can't, you can't, you can't . . .

I reconciled myself to the fact that a view from the distance was all I was going to get. Here I was in beautiful countryside on a warm, clear, sunny day. My little boy had slept in the car and was in a sweet mood, and I owed it to him as well as to myself to shake off the grey fog that seems permanently to fill your head after months of sleep deprivation. It was the kind of day for being glad to be alive, not for feeling disappointed. So we wandered around the sights of the village for a while and stopped at a little café for snacks, and then hopped back in the car and drove round winding roads to the top of the cliff to see the view.

From the lookout point at the top of the gorge the scene lay below us in exquisite beauty, the chapel buildings on their rocky promontory seeming to be carved into the rock itself, with the town laid out on the slopes below. Immediately to our left a mud path emerged which snaked up the hillside from the chapels, and up the path, fresh from their visit to the Black Madonna, came a steady stream of walkers with their sturdy shoes and sunhats and backpacks.

How I longed, just in that moment, to feel that free – to leave behind all the nappies and the feeding bottles and the sun parasols and the car, and simply walk all day and sleep all night. I hadn't had a full night's sleep in eighteen months, and my frazzled brain suddenly latched onto the idea that travelling light, walking long miles and sleeping at night would be heaven on earth. But as I watched the people walking up the path, slowly the longing for freedom began to crystallise into some kind of determination. Damn it. I might not be able to don a backpack and walk a hundred miles, but what was to stop me walking *down* this bit of the path, just as far as the chapels? The path was dry, easily wide enough for a pushchair and not too steep. The only real obstacle, apart from all the people coming in the other direction, was the chorus of 'you can't' that was replaying itself in my mind. I tried the first little slope, and it really was quite safe. The path zigzagged down the slope, and at each hairpin bend was a station of the cross, complete with tall, almost life-size chipped plaster figures with their faded paint and mournful faces. The stations, of course, were designed for people walking up, not down, so I observed the story of Jesus' last hours in reverse order. I carefully manoeuvred the pushchair down the path, taking many little breaks along the way and giving plenty of smiles and apologies to those who were walking up the path, until eventually we found ourselves in a shady courtyard called the Plateau of St Michel, from which various buildings opened outwards. Leaving the pushchair outside, I carried my son through the Basilique St-Saveur, a large, Romanesque-Gothic church laden with paintings and inscriptions of celebrated visitors. We made our way through the musty, incense-laden air, past the remains of an iron sword that, it's claimed, was Roland's sword Durandal, and through a small doorway into the Chapelle de Notre Dame. And there, within a highly ornate painted shrine, for the veneration of pilgrims and the curiosity of tourists, sat the Black Madonna.

Visiting a renowned work of art, people often imagine that its size will match its significance. But, like the *Mona Lisa*, the Black Madonna was much smaller than I expected. A fragile and bent little figure, quite touching in her simplicity, she looked surprisingly human and much older than a new mother ought to be. Unlike some Madonnas who seem so otherworldly as to be beyond changing a nappy or mixing a bottle of baby milk, the Black Madonna, despite having more the air of a grandmother, still seemed worldly enough to know a thing or two about looking after a baby. I looked at her for a few minutes, wondering at the weight of expectations that had been loaded on this little figure – centuries of hoped-for healings, countless longings for a child – and once again felt a great wave of gratitude for my own beautiful, complicated son.

The best part of the shrine complex, though, was not the ornate chapels, nor even the Madonna, but the sun-dappled courtyard. Warm, safe and enclosed on all sides, it had an almost womb-like atmosphere, and I sat on the steps in the shade as my son plodded about on his toddler's legs. He laughed as he jumped in and out of the shadows and seemed quite at peace with his world, and as I sat there and closed my eyes it was as if the fragments of my soul started to come back together. I could see that I wouldn't be walking any kind of journey with unfettered freedom for a long time to come. All children need their parents, and I had a baby with more needs than most, so the space to be just myself, by myself, without constantly looking out for someone else, was some distance into the future. But what did that matter, really? I had been given what so many had prayed to the Madonna for, what I myself had longed for, and despite the chorus of voices that said 'you can't', here we were anyway.

Perhaps, like motherhood, pilgrimage occurs despite imperfect circumstances and inconvenient timing. Perhaps, like motherhood, there is really no set of rules that qualifies you to be a pilgrim. Perhaps there are as many ways of being a pilgrim as there are of being a mother. But for me, at any rate, I couldn't be one apart from the other.

Later, as we wound our way back up the dusty path to the top of the hill, this time going with the flow of traffic, it occurred to me that I had been thinking of pilgrimage in terms of the place, but the real point is what happens to the pilgrim.

Then I remembered what I had learned in Jerusalem. From what we know of the earliest Christian communities, there is little to indicate that they made pilgrimages in the same way that later generations did, and rather than travelling to specific holy places to carry out votive rituals or healing prayers, there seems to have been more emphasis on the idea of life itself as a journey.

The resurrection and the coming of the Holy Spirit at Pentecost had brought about the belief not only that they lived in a new era in which God was present with them, but also that another enormous change was imminent with the expected return of Christ, heralding the beginning of a new age when both earth and heaven would be renewed. This wasn't an escapist vision – they didn't simply expect to be transported to eternal bliss. Rather the hope was that this world too would be transformed into a place of peace and justice.[6]

In the meantime, however, many of them were living through intense persecution as well as constant political unrest, and the hope of Christ's return gave the strength to endure horrifying torture and constant insecurity. But it's also worth considering that communities which live constantly under threat do lose, to some extent, their sense of rootedness or connection to their home, and instead have an acute awareness of the temporary quality of life – something which is also likely to have contributed to their concept of life as a journey towards something else.

The threat of persecution also had a practical effect on their relationship to ritual and sacred space, because in order to avoid being found at worship they often met in secret locations such as the catacombs, or in people's homes, rather than in public places. The combination, then, of a psychological unrootedness and a constant fear for personal safety made the hope of heaven and better things to come seem not just a far-off promise, but an acute reality.

There was an urgency in those early days of Christian faith to be ready at all times for the return of Christ – perhaps next month or next week, perhaps even tomorrow – and not miss the moment when it happened. The hope of heaven, and the idea of being a pilgrim through life, was constantly used to motivate Christians to continue the challenging walk of faith they had begun. Life on earth, said the New Testament writers, was a journey towards something far better, and precisely because they were 'strangers and pilgrims' (see 1 Peter 2:11 KJV) they should keep their eyes on the prize and not be distracted by physical appetites or temporary worries. The author of the letter to the Hebrews used the example of Old Testament heroes to encourage his church:

> These all died in faith, not having received the prom-
> ises, but having seen them afar off, and were persuaded
> of them, and embraced them, and confessed that they
> were strangers and pilgrims on the earth. (Heb. 11:13
> KJV)

For both practical and theological reasons, therefore, the early Christians thought of themselves as 'citizens of heaven', belonging to a place that was yet to be brought fully into reality, and thus they were sojourners in this world. While they aimed to live responsibly and respectfully in their civic communities, they held very lightly what they regarded as temporary and less 'real' than their spiritual identity, and maintained their loyalty to the heavenly kingdom. Mathetes wrote to Diognetus in about AD 200:

Christians dwell in their own countries, but simply as sojourners. As citizens, they share in all things with others, and yet endure all things as if foreigners. Every foreign land is to them as their native country, and every land of their birth as a land of strangers . . . They pass their days on earth, but they are citizens of heaven.[7]

But although this may have meant that the kind of journeys we associate with pilgrimages were unfamiliar to them, by constantly treating their homeland as a temporary camping space, they maintained a mobile, nomadic view of their life on earth. Christianity, in the early centuries, was not for those who wanted to settle down or make their home their castle.

'We should keep it constantly in mind', wrote Cyprian, Bishop of Carthage (249–58), 'that we have renounced the world, and that we sojourn here for a time as strangers and foreigners.'[8]

St Augustine, too, approached the difficulties of life by holding in tension the idea of heaven and earth as two parallel worlds. After the Goths sacked Rome in 410 he wrote *Concerning the City of God against the Pagans* in which he contrasts an earthly city, where Christian faith was counter-cultural to the beliefs and values of heathen society, with the city of heaven where, they believed, their future life would be free of such contradictions.[9] Augustine urged his readers towards a pilgrim mentality, to travel light and not be weighed down or distracted by earthly possessions, for this world was nothing more than a temporary stopping place en route to the heavenly city.

No one with a child under five can possibly claim to travel light. But driving back from Rocamadour that evening, it was clear to me that there was one particular piece of mental baggage I needed to jettison in order to lighten the spiritual and emotional load, and not feel so bogged down in all the different roles I had to juggle. It was time to stop the endless chorus of 'you can't' playing like a broken record in my head. I smiled to myself as I thought of our back-to-front pushchair pilgrimage. I could imagine various people I knew dismissing our little trip as not being a 'real' pilgrimage. And – technically – I guess they would have been right. But it seemed rather wonderful to me that, against the odds, we had found our way to the Black Virgin, realised that the untidiness of a mother-and-child situation was precisely what she represented, and in the clear shafts of light streaming into the courtyard somehow had reconnected with joy and goodness.

'You can't go on a pilgrimage with a baby,' I heard the voices say.

I glanced in the rear-view mirror and smiled at my son, dozing off in his car seat in the back. And out loud, I said, 'We can, Ben. We really can.'

After the joy and liberation of my not-quite-pilgrimage to Rocamadour, I was ready to plan a few more trips. It was not my intention simply to overthrow previous ideas of pilgrimage and make up my own rules: after all, a good set of rules, put in place by someone who has trodden the path before, should function both to protect and enable, save you from wasting a lot of time and ensure you get the most out of your endeavour. But when rules become a straitjacket instead of a liberation it's time to revisit them to find out what's gone awry. I couldn't help but think that if pilgrimage could include wheelchairs at Lourdes, there shouldn't be anything that extraordinary about a pushchair. But I was less sure whether a pilgrimage should be fun. Does it always have to be a serious endeavour, marked by penance and sober reflection, or is there room for joy in a pilgrimage? Christian doctrine tells us that joy is one of the fruits of the Holy Spirit, yet do we dare to believe it? Joy and pleasure are not the same thing, but it would be a mistake to think that joy is only true joy if you don't enjoy it too much. And while some hedonistic pleasures may be ultimately destructive, there is no virtue in being miserable. Many of life's pleasures are not destructive but life-giving – eating and drinking with friends, laughter, playing or listening to great music, dancing, love, sex – these can all be used recklessly, but they are not bad in themselves. Christianity really doesn't do itself any favours by turning virtue into the equivalent of a pinched, joyless existence, and there is really no basis for doing so either in Christian doctrine or in the biblical record – the opposite, in fact. The Psalms display the full range of emotional responses to life; grief is met with tears and injustice with white-hot anger, but joy is welcomed with open arms. It seemed reasonable, then, to expect that joy might enter into the pilgrimage experience. Little did I know, however, that my next journey was to be not merely joyful, but would have a distinct comedy element.

I was holidaying on the coast of Norfolk which, while it can hardly be described as geographically remote, does feel somewhat out of the way since it isn't on the way to anywhere else: the only reason you go there is to go there. The north Norfolk beaches are some of the most beautiful in Britain, and on a sunny day in the summer you need nothing more than a spot on the beach, a bucket and spade or a good book and a picnic basket to be entirely happy. Even in the winter, as long as you are wrapped up warm against the elements it's the perfect place for a good stomp along the shore. But there are some delightful places inland too, one of which is the small town of Walsingham. In 1061, during the reign of Edward the Confessor, Richelda, the widow of the Lord of Walsingham Manor, had a dream in which she was transported to the house in Nazareth where the Angel Gabriel had announced to Mary that she was to be the mother of Christ. Richelda had the same dream three times and became convinced that she should build a replica of the house. This she did (although another embellishment of the legend says that local workmen inexplicably found it impossible to build the house, so Richelda spent an entire night praying and in the morning it was found that the Holy House in Nazareth had miraculously been transported to Walsingham). Being a Marian shrine, it soon became one of England's most visited sites, rivalling even Canterbury in popularity and drawing pilgrims from all over England and Europe. King Henry III had a particular fondness for the Virgin Mary and in around 1226 made the first of many pilgrimages to Walsingham, after which he gave the canons his royal patronage. From then until the dissolution of the priory in 1538, nearly every English monarch visited Walsingham, including Henry VIII and Catherine of Aragon.

By tradition, medieval pilgrims would pause about a mile south of Walsingham at Houghton St Giles, a small hamlet where the Slipper Chapel stands on the roadside. Built in the mid-fourteenth century, the chapel was dedicated to St Catharine of Alexandria, whose tomb lies within the monastery on Mount Sinai built on the spot where Moses took off his shoes when he found himself standing on holy ground. St Catharine was the patron saint of pilgrims to the Holy Land, and therefore an important figure for pilgrims travelling to the 'Nazareth' of England. Pilgrims who stopped at St Catharine's used to remove their footwear and walk barefoot the 'Holy Mile' from there to the shrine. In 1934 the Mass was celebrated at the Slipper Chapel for the first time since the Reformation, and four years later the building was reconsecrated, since when some have revived the old tradition of leaving their shoes there.

In the 1930s Walsingham underwent an enormous pilgrimage revival and now boasts chapels of many different denominations. At theological college I had encountered plenty of Walsingham enthusiasts who donned their cassocks every year to join in with organised pilgrimages, from the Student Cross pilgrimage at Easter to the great theatrical procession that draws thousands of pilgrims there each May. The day my son and I set off for Walsingham promised to be fairly quiet by comparison. I had planned to drive to the outskirts of the town and walk the Holy Mile (although probably with my shoes on), but then I discovered that a narrow-gauge railway ran all the way from the coast to the edge of Walsingham. This alternative means of transport seemed the perfect way to help a small boy enter into the experience, so I parked at Wells, bought a couple of tickets, folded up the buggy, and we climbed aboard.

The sun was shining in a clear blue sky as we left the coast, but the area is renowned for having very different coastal and inland weather conditions, and as we chugged along the temperature dropped, grey skies brooded and then the rain began to fall. The open-sided carriages gave little protection from the rain, so we were soon pretty wet, but it was only after we disembarked that the heavens really opened. Thoroughly drenched, my feet squelched in my shoes as I pushed the buggy towards the town. We stopped at a small café to shelter and warm up until the rain stopped, and then set off once again.

Fifteen minutes later there was another downpour, and this time I spotted a shop across the road with a large window display that appeared to be full of children's toys. It wasn't until we were at the door that I realised it was, in fact, a clerical vestments shop (affectionately known to the clergy as a 'tat shop'). Here you can go to purchase robes or incense, baptism certificates and Bibles, and all the sundries required to keep a church ticking over. Even after more than a decade in the world of Church wonders, I am amazed by the fact that the style of shirt or cassock or robe is chosen, not principally because it fits you, or is machine washable or easy to iron, but because of the theological message that the garments are deemed to carry. Even all those tiny buttons are invested with meaning – one for each of the 39 Articles of the Church of England. According to vestry folklore, a priest might express a quiet rebellion against one or other of the Articles by leaving the corresponding button undone.

We dived into the tat shop for shelter, and while we waited for the rain to stop were highly entertained by the hilarious religious kitsch, which I had mistaken for toys, that filled the windows and shelves of the shop. A picture of Jesus hanging on the cross, turned first one way and then the other, could alternately be seen to look pleadingly up to heaven and then appear with closed eyes and tears running down his face. There was a plastic Jesus to hang from your rear-view mirror, and another that was the religious equivalent of a nodding dog for the back shelf of a car, with Jesus' arms raised and lowered in blessing (or possibly waving his finger at you in rebuke). My son was fascinated by a statue of the Virgin that had an inner light that could be switched on and off. But best of all was a pale green plastic glow-in-the-dark Virgin Mary. There was something incongruous about the juxtaposition of these tacky ornaments with the rails of ceremonial robes, one side of the shop bearing witness to the fact that on one level the Church takes herself and her rituals far too seriously, while this odd collection of kitsch showed the Church with a sense of humour, quite at home with sending herself up.

At last the rain stopped for good, and as the sun broke through we found our way back to the road and began to visit some of the many denominational chapels which, on the surface at least, seem to exist fairly happily side by side.

The Anglican shrine is built around the Holy House itself
(which has been rebuilt a number of times since Richelda's
day). I quickly found the Chapel of the Ascension, which is
renowned for its ceramic decoration. In the white ceiling
there is what at first appears to be a ceiling rose, but on closer
inspection you discover that instead of a light fitting there
are, protruding from the centre, two plaster feet, complete
with nail holes, creating the idea that Jesus is disappearing
into the clouds. Had I been in a more serious mood, perhaps
I might have imagined myself, like the disciples, looking up
into the heavens as Jesus disappeared from sight. But after a
shop full of flashing, bowing, winking and glow-in-the-dark
icons, and helped along by the incredulity of a three-year-old
wondering why there were two feet in the ceiling, rather than
being inspired to pray I collapsed in giggles.

It was impossible to miss the more sombre side of the
pilgrimage experience in some of the other corners of the
church. Around the walls were posted a multitude of prayer
requests on slips of paper. Many of them simply had names
written on them, while others asked for healing from dread
diseases, or for strength to cope with bereavement. It was
hard not to feel touched by the weight of human need in this
place. This wasn't just a theatrical spectacle or a superstitious
ritual, but the evidence of real people, some in quiet desperation, searching for a shaft of light in their darkest hour. We lit
a couple of candles to pray for people we loved, and to add a
prayer of solidarity with all those who had prayed there in
their hour of need. But despite that I still felt, in that instant,
more like a visitor observing someone else's pilgrimage. Even

though I was touched by their need, this place felt culturally alien to me.

As we strolled from one chapel to another, the lightness and humour of the morning seemed to recede and I began to feel a little oppressed by the excessive religious clutter. Why, I wondered, when some of the greatest art in the world has a religious theme, do so many churches end up full of such low-quality religious artefacts? Theologian David Brown has argued that even through bad art, God can and will speak. God, he says, is no respecter of good taste. Brown may be right, and in any case it wasn't for me to sit in judgement over those who found a connection to the divine through what appeared to me to be a rather tacky statue. All the same, from a purely personal perspective, the effect of an over-abundance of bad art, ecclesiastical clutter and mournful plaster figures in a dark and secluded space was having a depressing effect.

The morning's deluge had given way to an unpredictably beautiful late afternoon, and there was one thing left to visit in Walsingham – the abbey gardens. After Richelda built Walsingham's Holy House, a priory was founded by the Augustinians in 1153. Nearly four hundred years later, at the dissolution of the monasteries, the priory was largely demolished. Another century after that, in the 1640s, Bishop John Warner bought the ruins and the surrounding farmland, later making a gift of the property to his nephew, Archdeacon Lee. Lee's family built a large house on the property which incorporated the ruins of the prior's lodgings, the infirmary and some of the outhouses. The house is still occupied, but the grounds are open to visitors.

I bought our tickets, moved fairly swiftly through the exhibition and out into the gardens where all that remains of the Priory Church is the tall, elegant arch of the East Window, beautiful in its simplicity and standing as an anchor into history. The sunlight was catching on the wet grass, and all around the ruins and along the paths to the river were clumps of summer flowers.

Again, seeing the scene through my son's eyes lifted the picture onto a new plane. Jesus once said that in order to grasp what the kingdom of God is all about, you need to be like a little child. I have never been much persuaded that he was talking about innocence: the real gift of seeing things through the eyes of a child is the ability to live in the present. No matter what a day has brought thus far, it seems to take a three-year-old less than half a minute to switch back into a happy mood once the sun is shining. Wandering in and out of the ancient arch and exploring the steps to the ancient refectory, he treated these dignified ruins as curiosities and playthings. It took me a little longer to adjust, but I let his happy mood lead the way for mine and gradually, with the sun on my back and the beauty of the garden, I felt the sombre mood of the churches slip away and a sense of lightness and hopefulness returned.

I was beginning to spot a pattern here. I am not one of life's naturally religious people. Although I don't object to religious practices, I am not most at home with elaborate robes and incense, the dark corners of musty chapels and the chipped plaster of the venerated saints. I remembered something Coleridge had written as a young man in his *Lectures on*

Religion. Using stained-glass windows as a metaphor for the Church, he delivered a pretty excoriating attack on the hypocrisy of those within the Church hierarchy who used their power to maintain the status quo. Stained-glass windows, he said, with their pictures of Gospel stories, were supposed to bring truth and illumination; instead they served only to keep out the light, obfuscating the clear, fresh air of God's goodness. I had certainly not experienced an abuse of power in Walsingham, but the buildings did represent a form of religion that was not very accepting of women and culturally left me feeling like an outsider.

I didn't feel any need to criticise what I saw, or the people who like that kind of religion; I simply needed to admit to myself that there are forms of church that prove more of a hindrance than a help to me. I am not much at home in the strictures and rigid rules of reformed evangelicalism which seem to demand a spirituality without beauty and a life with no spontaneity, and neither does my heart lift to the excessively theatrical, ritualised liturgies of Anglo-Catholicism. The smoky patina, musty fabrics and chaotic clutter make me restless, and the underlying objections to women's participation in church life leave me feeling desperate for some fresh air. It would be easy to conclude that I am not cut out for Christian spirituality at all, except for the fact that there are thousands of others like me who, despite feeling like a fish out of water with many aspects of the tradition, still align themselves with the goodness and justice of Jesus of Nazareth, engage with the hope of salvation through the story of the resurrection and are not afraid to make considerable sacrifices in order to belong to a community of like-minded people. Any believer is bound to live with a degree of paradox. On the one hand faith needs to be countercultural to some degree, for a religion that gives itself every excuse to conform to the culture around it is likely to have so little substance that it may as well not be followed at all. Every few generations, faith shifts a little to negotiate a path that neither slavishly conforms to the tradition, nor caves in to a secularised future. The core of this faith is a hope that springs out of the trope of resurrection: the future is not a downward spiral, but rings with a clarity of promise at the same time as being shrouded in mystery.

Joy, then, had surfaced once again in this pilgrimage that turned out to be something of a comedy of errors. Despite starting out in a deluge, and not feeling drawn in by the chapels and churches, playing in the abbey gardens I discovered a deep sense of peace and happiness that seemed a perfect fit. I was glad to have been there, and even more glad to have discovered that even in Walsingham there is a place for people like me who don't naturally gravitate to the Gothic theatricality that some of her buildings project. Summer flowers growing among the remains of an ancient abbey seemed a good alternative metaphor to Coleridge's oppressive stained glass. Miniature railways and glow-in-the-dark Virgins notwithstanding, I was touched by the hope of the resurrection, not as an intellectual problem, but as a spiritual beckoning simply to live the life I have.

Later I wondered why it is that religion can produce a sense of obligation to tone down emotion. Why is goodness thinned down to a kind of limp worthiness, peace to a bland numbness rather than a deep sense of absolute satisfaction, and joy nothing much more than a beatific smile? Irenaeus famously wrote, 'For the glory of God is a human being fully alive, and the life of humanity consists in the vision of God.'[10] If faith makes us fully alive, then surely it ought to include the kind of happiness you get from working really hard and finishing a job well, love that absorbs you completely and costs everything you have, a peace that delivers a deep and restful sleep, and the kind of laugh-out-loud celebratory joy that comes with good news or quick-witted humour. And as for goodness, it should be far from the kind of goody-two-shoes smugness that (mysteriously to me, who could never quite manage to produce it) always seemed to please headmistresses. True goodness is a matter of joy, not of extreme, stoical self-restraint, or an appearance of innocence that masks a ton of attitude. But dare we believe in a depth of true goodness that pervades life and makes a foundation of trust and stability upon which all kinds of adventures can be founded? One group of pilgrims who seemed to know something about the recovery of joy were the Celtic monks who embarked on extraordinary journeys and who are often referred to as *peregrini*.

The word *peregrinus*, in classical Latin, didn't necessarily refer to a person travelling to a sacred place; it simply meant a wanderer, a traveller, someone far from home, or a stranger in town.[11] In the Latin Vulgate Jesus is described as a *peregrinus* in Luke 24 when the two disciples on the Emmaus Road, failing to recognise him, wonder how this apparent stranger can possibly be in Jerusalem and not know about the death of Jesus just two days earlier. So '. . . *ei tu solus peregrinus es in Hierusalem et non cognovisti quae facta sunt in illa his diebus*' translates as, 'Are you the only visitor to Jerusalem who doesn't know what has happened here recently?' or, 'Are you so new in town that you don't know what's happened?'

Peregrinus, though, had a certain flexibility of meaning. In medieval ecclesiastical terminology a 'pilgrim' was someone who left his or her ordinary occupation for a time to make a specific journey to a sacred place, while a 'palmer' was someone who made a lifestyle of constant wandering. Dante gave his own particular flourish to the definition of the terms: 'Pilgrim may be understood in the broad sense, in so far as whoever is outside his fatherland is a pilgrim; in the narrow sense none is called a pilgrim save him who is journeying towards the sanctuary of St James or returning from it . . .'[12]

The Celtic monks who are usually referred to as *peregrini* were pilgrims more in the sense of permanent wanderers, but they gave their own unique spin to the idea. Rather than setting out towards a specific destination, they took the New Testament description of Christians as 'strangers and pilgrims' quite literally, renouncing family and home to make their *peregrinatio pro amore Dei* ('pilgrimage for the love of God'). Just as the Desert Fathers had gone into exile, the Celtic *peregrini* sought out places where they could battle against the darkness in their own version of the wilderness

– sometimes on land, sometimes on islands that were 'deserts in the ocean', and sometimes in a unique kind of pilgrimage journey in which they set out on sea voyages with neither map nor compass. Thinking that they would literally fling themselves upon the mercy of God, they put out to sea in coracles, abandoning themselves to the waves in the belief that God would not only protect them, but would take them wherever he wished.

This may sound adventurous or even reckless, but the idea behind it was consciously to cut oneself off from the comforts of home and the safety of dry land, and to test one's own faith in God (this, of course, being in a time long before there was any air rescue, so the sea was even more perilous than it is now). Setting out without any plan or means of navigation, they regarded the chaos of the sea as the wilderness in which their souls would be tested, believing that only if God willed it would they be safely returned to dry land.

St Brendan is said to have sailed in this way on a seven-year voyage that began in Ireland and eventually led him across the Atlantic to America, in the company of a boat full of pilgrims who trusted entirely in God's providence to guide them to shore. This was the prayer he spoke before leaving:

> Shall I abandon, O King of mysteries, the soft comforts of home?
> Shall I turn my back on my native land, and turn my face towards the sea?
> Shall I put myself wholly at Your mercy, without silver, without a horse, without fame, without honour?

Shall I throw myself wholly upon You, without sword
and shield, without food and drink, without a bed to
lie on?

Shall I say farewell to my beautiful land, placing myself
under Your yoke?

Shall I pour out my heart to You, confessing my
manifold sins and begging forgiveness, tears
streaming down my cheeks?

Shall I leave the prints of my knees on the sandy
beach, a record of my final prayer in my native land?

Shall I then suffer every kind of wound that the sea can
inflict?

Shall I take my tiny boat across the wide sparkling ocean?

O King of the Glorious Heaven, shall I go of my own
choice upon the sea?

O Christ, will You help me on the wild waves?

Brendan's prayer expresses beautifully the fact that even for those who feel a call to a particular way of pursuing spiritual life, there is still an element of choice involved in how we develop our own faith: choosing adventure comes with genuine risks and at the cost of certain comforts, but we are not obliged to go the difficult route. Launching out into the deep not knowing where they would end up, the *peregrini* were not tourists or day-trippers, but risk-takers who threw themselves uncompromisingly into life's adventure, believing it was a choice worth making. Brendan's legend suggests that when he did eventually come to land in America, he took it as his destiny, believing that God had guided him there.

The Celtic *peregrini* seemed to speak volumes to my push-chair pilgrimages, not because my little voyages were particularly dangerous, but because rethinking one's life in the new set of circumstances that motherhood brings is, in some respects, a journey of unpredictability that involves the loss of control over one's own life and destiny. Although I experienced motherhood (and still do) as a gift and an adventure, there have been times along the way when I have been overcome with a feeling of being profoundly lost. I was used, in my profession, to being treated as a competent person, so it was unsettling to find that in some corners of the world – maternity wards and primary school playgrounds being the worst offenders – mothers are regarded as brain-less, powerless and unworthy of an opinion on anything, not even on a child you know better than anyone else and for whom you would lay down your life. The *peregrini*, then, voyaging through uncharted waters, seemed to me an apt image for this particular part of my life, with its unexpected moments of lostness.

Rudy must re-enter the story here, for it is one of his unshakable beliefs that deliberately allowing yourself to get lost is an excellent way of having an adventure. It sounds like a plausible theory, but in practice, getting lost can also be a guaranteed way of having a miserable time trying to find your way back off a rocky outcrop while missing something stun-ning a mere half a mile away that you would have found had you bothered to bring the map along. The only two times I have ever fallen out with Rudy were over his determination not to read the map. I discovered his attachment to the idea of a mapless adventure on the trip to Israel when, on a free day, we agreed that we should head for the middle of Jerusalem and set out to see things that so far we had missed.

'Right,' I said, as the bus sped towards the city. 'We have a whole day – where do you want to go? There are at least four things Joe mentioned yesterday that we haven't seen yet. Pass the map and we can make a plan.'

'I didn't bring the map,' he said. 'I thought it would be a great opportunity to get lost and have a real adventure.' I was dumbfounded, certain that two naïve-looking Westerners (both of us white-skinned and fair-haired types who stand out in a crowd anywhere outside northern Europe) ought to know where they were going and which parts of an unfamiliar city it might be smart to give a wide berth to. After several hot, fruitless hours toiling around grubby backstreets, we finally had a little showdown. I bought another map and made a plan. He thought me woefully unadventurous.

Several years later, when I was six months pregnant with my son, I was on a summer holiday in North Wales with a group of friends, including Rudy who had brought his dog with him. One day the eight of us drove to Snowdon, the plan being for me to go up the mountain in the little railway while everyone else walked. But as we arrived, Rudy suddenly announced that he would go up in the train to keep me company. We strolled over to the train, only to find that dogs were not allowed on board. Reluctant to spoil Rudy's day, I urged him to catch up with the others and leave me to look after myself. But Rudy said he wouldn't hear of it – we could find something else to do, he said, like drive to a nearby castle instead.

'You're too kind,' I said as we walked back to the car. 'There was really no need to stay down here with me.'

Rudy looked completely baffled. 'No need? Look at yourself! What if something went wrong? You'd be all by yourself in rural Wales with no one to help. There's no way I was leaving you on your own.'

We drove off to a nearby village with a castle and dozens of tea rooms, and had a splendid day pottering around, stopping for plenty of rests for my benefit. In the middle of the afternoon we went back to the car to drive to the holiday cottage. Suddenly Rudy's sense of adventure descended like a daemon. He took a turning to the right down a little unmarked road, and my heart sank as he began to muse out loud that it looked rather interesting, and he wondered where it might lead. But how could I complain? This was my friend who had given up his day of mountain walking to save me from being alone. It was only fair to indulge him in his little adventurous moment.

Half an hour later we were well and truly lost, far from the main road with no landmarks in view and no road signs. My back began to ache, the baby was kicking and punching for all his life's worth, and I was beginning to feel a lot less mellow.

'I want to go back now,' I said.

'But we might be really close to the sea! It can't be that far away, surely.'

'I don't care about the sea any more, we're just hopelessly lost and I'm not enjoying it.'

'Oh, come on,' said Rudy, 'where's your sense of adventure? Look at the landscape, feel the sense of freedom!'

'Damn your sense of freedom,' I snapped, in an uncharacteristically fierce moment. 'My back hurts! A lot! Read the map and drive me home. Right! Now!'

'Sorry,' said Rudy, philosophically. 'I thought it would be fun. I put the map in the boot so we wouldn't be tempted to look. I'll stop just the second we're over this hill and get it out. Promise. No more surprises.'

Over the hill we drove, and suddenly the road fell away before us to a stunning panorama of rocky coastline dotted with tiny pink flowers, and beyond the cliffs, as far as the eye could see, stretched the bluest of navy blue seas. It would have been a lovely sight to see even if we had planned it, but happening upon it by surprise as we came over the crest of the hill made it a moment of heart-stopping beauty. Rudy stopped the car and we walked onto the cliffs and looked out towards the horizon. There was a stiff breeze, the late afternoon sun caught on the choppy waves so that they sparkled like diamonds, and high above the water circled some seabirds, their white wings catching the light. Stretching out in the fresh air, I felt better, and was glad after all that we hadn't missed this extraordinary sight. Perhaps Rudy was right: allowing yourself to get lost once in a while opens you up to experience the world in new ways and recaptures the element of surprise and wonder that in childhood is an everyday experience, but is so easy to lose when you grow up.

Rudy's enjoyment of getting lost and that moment of discovery on the Welsh coast came sharply to mind as I read about the *peregrini*. It has been a recent trend in Christian spirituality to speak of life as a journey – so much so that it has almost become a cliché – but in a significantly different sense from the way it was used at earlier stages in Christian history. For the early Christians under persecution there were often occasions when life must have seemed cheap, and the hope of heaven a blessed relief by comparison. Move forward a few centuries, and Brendan's prayer suggests that while the *peregrini* also had their eyes on heaven as their ultimate destination, they consciously weighed up the benefits of life at home against the possibilities of a grand spiritual adventure. But in the modern world, at least in places where religious persecution is not part of daily experience, to conceive of life as a journey is not to treat it as a waiting room for heaven, or a trial to be survived while we wait for the afterlife. Living in the comfort of the West, we are less in need of the hope of a promised future to galvanise ourselves against the intense struggles of everyday life, and more inclined to think of a spiritual journey as something to be relished – like a lengthy, exploratory walk during which faith is gradually stretched and developed through daily experience in the company of friends, or perhaps, for those with more of a sense of adventure, the image of the *peregrini* jumping into a coracle and hanging on for dear life is more appealing.

Compared to the early Christians, our faith is far less a test of endurance; massive changes in our understanding of cosmology mean that our concept of heaven can no longer be a simplistic, literal expectation of a better world beyond the clouds, and for most people it is thankfully no longer the case that they subject themselves to an authoritarian Church for fear of later being cast into outer darkness. So our concept of heaven is less urgent, less concrete and less frightening, whereas life seems more of a gift.

In today's language, when we speak of pilgrimage either literally as a physical journey or metaphorically as a description of a life of faith, the emphasis has shifted to the journey itself rather than the destination. Ask any present-day pilgrim about their experience and, rather than talking about saints or shrines, they are more likely to wax lyrical about the route they travelled, the people they met along the way, the impact of the rhythm of the walk, how the pilgrimage made them think differently about their life and what effect it continued to have once they returned home. In fact, so powerful is the process of walking a lengthy pilgrimage that large numbers of people without any particular faith commitment now undertake the classic medieval journeys for the experience of the walk itself. As Robert Louis Stevenson put it, 'to travel hopefully is a better thing than to arrive',[13] or in the words of a Taoist saying, 'The journey is the reward.'

While it's true that this attitude is common in modern-day pilgrimage, that's not to say the value of the journey itself was entirely lost on our medieval forebears. History rarely divides ideas up quite as neatly as we would like to suppose, and the different ways of thinking about pilgrimage are not mutually exclusive. In particular, if we revisit *The Canterbury Tales* we might see that Harry Bailly had some influence on raising the significance of the journey.

On their first evening together, Chaucer's pilgrims ate supper in Bailly's tavern, and it was he who persuaded them to turn the journey into a story-telling competition. Each character would tell two stories on the way to Canterbury, and two on the way back; Bailly himself would accompany them on their journey, and be the judge of the competition, and at the end of it he would reward the best story-teller with a free meal in his tavern.

Bailly was clearly a shrewd businessman, for having already collected payment from this large group of travellers for one meal, his competition guaranteed that the whole company – apart from the prize-winner – would pay to eat there again on their return. The profits would easily have covered Bailly's own travelling expenses. A free holiday and extra income for persuading the travellers to follow his scheme? A modern-day travel agent would surely be impressed.

By setting them the challenge of telling their stories to pass the time, Harry Bailly redefined pilgrimage as being more about the journey than the destination. You could view this focus on the social aspects of pilgrimage negatively. But by assuming the place of judge and overseer of the group, Bailly's role in the tales becomes metaphorical of divine authority, which makes it all the more interesting that he is the one who broadens the capacity of pilgrimage from a stoical commitment to penance, pain, suffering and paying for your own sins, and instead authenticates its capacity for joy, humour, entertainment and human companionship.

The Harry Bailly approach to travel perhaps also forbids us from over-spiritualising pilgrimage, reminding us instead that such a journey not only removes you from home comforts, but also forces you into the constant company of others. Daily life usually gives us the luxury of limiting the hours per week we spend with each of our family, friends, co-workers and fellow worshippers. Pilgrimage, though, which generally has more in common with budget travel and youth hostels than with five-star accommodation and taxis, brings you close to fellow travellers – sometimes uncomfortably so, for some dither about while others stride ahead like sergeant-majors, barking instructions to others to keep up. And there are plenty who snore, talk too much, don't talk at all, hog the shower, or have various other annoying habits. And, of course, it doesn't take long to realise that you yourself are being seen close up by others. Any false impression created of noblesse or spiritual maturity is soon whittled away until the true picture becomes visible, but more often than not, in the midst of this dose of human reality there emerges a deepening sense of affection for, and dependence upon, others. Not for nothing did Chaucer name his characters a 'company' of pilgrims. 'Company' literally means 'with bread': a group of people who eat together develop a deeper and truer sense of relationship than those who remain in the safety of a formal distance.

Perhaps modern-day travel could do with a dose of Harry Bailly's earthy wisdom. We think of holidays as times to relax and regenerate, but travel is not always a restful pursuit: it's often reported that going on holiday is one of the most stressful events of our year, particularly if we get caught up in delays at airports or stations. We tend to think of a holiday beginning after we arrive at the destination – and understandably so, for who would want to count twenty-one hours in an airport delay as a holiday? Nevertheless, there may be a

case for shifting our mental attitude towards travel and treating the journey itself as part of the experience, for – as with
pilgrimage – travelling is one of those experiences that can
reveal our inner selves.

But perhaps these lessons can be inverted; perhaps they
might call us not only to set time aside to make beautiful
walks to magnificent places with a spiritual and social purpose,
but also to review the value of everyday journeys and the way
in which we approach them. For just as Chaucer gave us the
human underbelly of pilgrimage, showing his characters –
with all due affection and humour – to be thoroughly human
and full of flaws, so too the route they followed is a lot less
romantic than the medieval pastoral scenes I had once
imagined.

As a teenager I spent many summer holidays in the south of
England and took many walks along the chalk paths popularly
known as the Pilgrims Way that wind their way across the North
Downs through Surrey and Sussex. These paths are thought to
have originated as the tracks of Paleolithic hunters, but coins
from the fifth century BC found along the tracks suggest that by
pre-Roman times they had developed into a major trade route.
While other roads across clay would have been impassable for
much of the year, these chalk slopes stretching across the Downs
from Winchester to Canterbury and on to Dover, the main
English port, provided a good route for transporting tin, lead
and iron mined in the West Country.

Whether or not the paths were really used by medieval
pilgrims on their way to Canterbury is a matter of debate.
Christopher John Wright has argued that during the twelfth

century when Winchester's importance as a capital city declined, that section of the pathway probably fell into disuse as a trade route, and without medieval pilgrims the road would have disappeared.[14] But others point out that merchants and travellers might have used the paths in order to avoid the newer toll roads. There is no clear evidence that the title 'Pilgrims Way' was used any earlier than the eighteenth century, and in *The Old Road* (1904), Hilaire Belloc stated that the name referred only to the part of the pathway that runs between Winchester and Canterbury, not the entire network of paths. But even if its name was a romantic addition, the Pilgrims Way still remains a popular route for walkers, and it was in this guise that I walked the ancient paths.

My own memories of walks on the North Downs are mostly of long, hot summer days, with a few flies buzzing about, when time seemed largely suspended. Meandering down the chalk paths as a young teenager, I fondly imagined myself to be walking (as I had, somewhat inaccurately, been told) in the footsteps of Chaucer's pilgrims. Much later I discovered that this could not have been the case, for plotting their progress from London to Canterbury, identifying as far as possible the stopping places mentioned in the *Tales*, it quickly becomes apparent that their route followed more or less the Roman road, Watling Street, now rather unromantically the A2 from London to Canterbury, and only in a few places does it coincide with the chalk paths. Just as a closer look at Chaucer gradually unmasks the typical pilgrim as comically flawed, so tracing their route places their journey in the gritty reality of heavily used roads, where travellers, animals and carts alike were likely to find themselves marooned in deep mud. Next time you find yourself delayed for hours in an airport, don't give in to the romantic idea that travel was a simpler pleasure in the pre-modern age.

To approach life as a journey, then, can take on different shades of meaning. More or less importance may be given to the destination or to points along the route, we may savour the moment as we travel, or endure the present by living, mentally at least, in the future. If, in undertaking such a journey, we discover something about ourselves, our world and the way we relate to fellow pilgrims; if, along the way, we learn patience with those who walk more slowly, tolerance to get along with people who are not at all like us and the ingenuity and determination to get to our destination despite setbacks along the way, then we have learned lessons for life that may not have come so readily had we stayed at home.

3

Armchair pilgrim

> There is no need to run to Rome or Jerusalem to look for
> [Jesus] there, but turn your thought into your own soul
> where he is hidden.
> *Walter Hilton, Scale of Perfection, Book I.49, 5*

> The mind is its own place, and in itself
> Can make a heav'n of hell, a hell of heav'n.
> *Milton, Paradise Lost*

Pilgrimage almost disappeared after the Reformation.
Shrines, churches and monasteries were destroyed, bringing
dramatic change to both the spiritual and the physical landscape. But the impulse to travel gradually found new
expression in cultural and historical tourism, and such journeys as the Grand Tour took the place of pilgrimage, making
the great cities of Europe the focus of attention. Exciting new
archaeological discoveries in the nineteenth century created
a new wave of interest in the Middle East; ancient civilisations
came to life and created new and vigorous debate concerning biblical history. Thomas Cook saw a great opportunity
and began taking parties of tourists to Jerusalem in 1869. By
the turn of the twentieth century he had given more than
twelve thousand people guided tours around the Holy Land,

satisfying their taste for adventure and tourism while also giving them some devotional teaching. Cook played a significant part in what gradually developed into a full-scale revival of pilgrimage. Catholic pilgrims visited Rome and Marian shrines such as Lourdes, Rocamadour and Fatima, while Protestants rediscovered the historical British sites – Iona and Lindisfarne, Walsingham, Canterbury and Durham, and many ancient cathedrals, some of which revived the medieval practice of issuing pilgrim badges.

After the Second World War the distinction between Catholic and Protestant spirituality became less sharp, and this was encouraged by the foundation of the Taizé community in France. Begun by Brother Roger, Taizé was set up as an interdenominational order whose express purpose was to foster friendship and unity between nations that had been at war. Thousands of Christians of all denominations now make a pilgrimage to Taizé every year.

The revival of pilgrimage went hand in hand with a renewed interest in the idea that place has a spiritual significance. Tracing back through Christian history, it was often the case that a Christian church or chapel was built over a site considered sacred by earlier pagan religions and at first, as the old religion was displaced, the emphasis shifted to the founder or patron saint. Twentieth-century Christianity, though, discovered a new interest in the importance of the place as well as the person.

The pilgrimage revival also appealed to many who had no particular religious affiliation, but who wanted to make the journey out of historical interest, to retreat from everyday life for a time, or to rediscover the sense of travelling slowly over-land. And for all kinds of would-be pilgrims, one route in particular has risen to the top of the list. Wherever you go you'll find someone who has walked the Camino – the long road through southern France and northern Spain that even-tually leads to Santiago de Compostela. Some walk from further north in France, or even all the way from Canterbury, but there are countless books by people who have walked the Camino, many of whom no sooner finish their journey than they begin to plan their next trip. One of the features of the Camino, it seems, is that it embodies the 'Harry Baillie' effect. People who have made the trip will, if pressed, mention their arrival at Santiago, but mostly they talk about the journey itself: the effect it had on them, the way they settled into a different rhythm of life, the physical discipline and hardships of the walk, the companions met along the way, the liberating discovery that they really could live for weeks on end with the minimum of possessions, and the kindness of strangers.

Santiago de Compostela is a city in Galicia which legend claims as the burial place of Santiago (St James), brother of St John and one of Jesus' original disciples. James, it is said, was the first to bring the message of Christianity to Spain, later returning to Judea. In AD 44 he was martyred at the hand of Herod Agrippa, and after his death two of James's disciples took his body and boarded a boat made of stone, with neither oars nor sails. Guided by angels, the boat floated miraculously on a week-long voyage across the Mediterranean, through the Strait of Gibraltar and north through the Atlantic until they reached Galicia. There they met a heathen queen who offered them a cart pulled by oxen to help them on their way, but no sooner had they climbed aboard than they realised they had been tricked, and the cart was in fact being pulled by wild bulls. Seeing their imminent danger, they prayed to St James and the bulls miraculously became gentle and compliant, leading them through the forest to a place called Libredon where they came to a decisive halt. The disciples took this as a sign that this was the divinely appointed place and buried St James there. His body was then forgotten until AD 813 when Pelayo, a religious hermit from Iberia, followed a shining star to the burial place and found St James's relics there.

At this point the legend begins to connect with history, for in the ninth century AD the Moors abandoned the remote north-western corner of Spain and Christianity was able to re-emerge. Once it became renowned as the burial place of St James, Santiago quickly found itself on the map of Europe, because the importance of any shrine was judged according to the status of the relics held there. To visit a holy site with relics was a bit like earning a ticket to heaven, and at Compostela, the presence of the almost complete relics of one of Jesus' favourite disciples made the tickets first class. People began to walk there via various trade routes and path-ways, but the route was hazardous as there was no complete road to Compostela. *The Pilgrims Guide*, a literary account of the walk through northern France to Santiago written by Aymeric Picaud,[1] mentions that in the early days the journey proved so difficult that some pilgrims turned back. Gradually, though, pathways and bridges were built and small villages were settled along the way to provide food and shelter for the pilgrims. The Benedictines at Cluny saw an opportunity and founded new monasteries and churches along the route. Then in 1189 the pope raised the prestige of the shrine by awarding it Holy Year status and this, combined with the fact that the Crusades made it too dangerous to walk to Jerusalem, soon made Compostela as popular as Jerusalem and Rome. By the end of the twelfth century pilgrims were travelling from far and wide to walk the Camino, so much so that it became a huge melting pot of cultures. According to Goethe, it was on the road to Compostela that Europe was born.

For as long as the Camino has been in existence, pilgrims walking the route have worn a scallop shell. No one is entirely sure why the shell was chosen, but stories abound to explain it, quite possibly invented retrospectively. Some say that before the advent of Christianity there was a local cult for the pagan goddess Venus, and the scallop shell was carried over from her tradition. Others say it's an icon of the regeneration of the soul that Santiago offers. Another great legend suggests that James's disciples arrived on the shores of Galicia just as a wedding was about to begin. The groom rode along the beach on horseback, but at the sight of the stone barque and its strange cargo the horse was distracted and, with the bridegroom still mounted, careered wildly into the sea. It seemed that both horse and groom would drown, but then the first of James's miracles occurred and they both re-emerged from the sea, safe and dry, but covered from head to foot in scallop shells.

The Camino fell into disuse after the Reformation and St James's bones were lost. When they were found again in 1878 a papal bull was issued to confirm that they were genuine, but by this time the pilgrim route was heavily overgrown, what little accommodation could be found along the way was damp and disease-ridden, and it wasn't unheard of for those attempting the route to fall ill and die. It wasn't until the mid-twentieth century that the pilgrimage revival gradually led to pilgrim shelters, hostels and cafés being opened all along the ancient route. Now the Camino is more accessible than ever before. People travel from all over the world to walk some part of the route, some starting only a few days' journey from Santiago, others taking weeks to walk through southern France, or even all the way from Canterbury.

⇌

For years I've wanted to walk the Camino. You need at least a week, and preferably quite a bit longer, to cover enough of the route to make it worthwhile and with the best will in the world, I didn't think it was an undertaking for a pushchair pilgrim. I had decided to wait until my son was old enough either to walk with me, or to do without me for a few weeks. By the spring of 2009 he was tall and strong enough to walk good distances carrying a small pack, but hadn't yet hit the adolescent moment when he didn't want to hang out with his mother. We had already walked up and down a couple of small mountains and covered miles and miles of beach walks together, so at last it seemed the dream could become a reality and our plan to walk a stretch of the Camino began to take shape.

We were in the midst of wearing in new boots and studying the maps when, in the early summer, I woke up one morning with a fever. For four or five days I had flu-like symptoms, but as the fever receded the burning joints did not and by the end of the week I still couldn't move without pain. Every joint from my neck to my toes was swollen and painful and I couldn't even get my feet into my shoes, let alone go for a walk. My doctor started out upbeat. 'Don't worry,' she said, 'it's probably just the after-effects of a virus and the chances are you'll be back to normal in a few weeks.'

By mid-summer, however, I was on a new kind of journey altogether as it became apparent that my body had turned on itself with an auto-immune arthritis. Somewhere in the future lay the promise that mobility would return, but it was clear I was in for a few months of tinkering with drugs and therapies and learning to manage the condition. Moving slowly and stiffly with burning pain in every joint, I reconciled myself to the fact that not only was walking the Camino postponed indefinitely, there would in fact be no summer holiday of any kind. I would be doing the gentlest of therapeutic exercises, sleeping a lot, and resting in between. Sitting in the armchair in my kitchen one morning, I looked at the two pairs of new boots standing on the shelf and decided that spending the summer feeling disappointed and angry wasn't going to help. I had no clear view forward as to what impact this illness would have on my life, but it clearly was not going away. Not only was I in for an enforced summer of staying in one place, I could also see that I might need to reimagine the next phase of my life on slightly different terms.

There are plenty of other would-be pilgrims and travellers who have suffered enforced immobility. One famous example is Ignatius of Loyola, a young soldier who was, by all accounts, an affected, ambitious and vain young man. His longing for glory was brought to a sudden halt when a cannonball damaged both his legs, one very badly. As the leg was treated he became critically ill, but once the crisis passed he found himself bedridden at his castle home in Loyola for a long convalescence. To pass the time he asked for some of his favourite books – tales of romantic chivalry in which knights and warriors would compete in love and war. There were no chivalric books in the castle, so instead he was offered the lives of Christ and the saints to divert him. He began by treating them like the chivalric tales, imagining himself as a knight in competition with the saints. 'Suppose I were to rival this saint in fasting, that one in endurance, that one in pilgrimages,' he mused, but then his thoughts would wander again to romance and heroic exploits.

After a while he began to notice a pattern: when he thought of chivalry he ended up feeling despondent, but when he meditated on the lives of the saints he found himself contented and joyful. Gradually he allowed his spiritual meditations to take precedence and then one night, according to his autobiography, he had a kind of vision of the child Jesus with his mother, which resulted in him renouncing his past life. Those around him began to notice the change his conversion had brought about, and they were not pleased. His brother, anxious that all this spiritual enthusiasm would reflect badly on the family, begged him to tone down his spiritual interests. But too late: Ignatius had discovered his own life's path, and the contrasting feelings of despondency and joy he had experienced in his convalescence formed the basis of the spiritual exercises for which he became famous and which are still widely practised today. Whatever brought peace and a deep-seated sense of well-being was, for Ignatius, a consolation and a sign of the Spirit of God. Whatever brought gloom and despondency was a desolation. He was not so simplistic as to suggest that the spiritual path simply avoids unhappiness: indeed, enduring some desolation was an inevitable part of seeking after God. But he was clear nonetheless that these shadowy feelings had to be carefully discerned and that deliberately seeking desolation was not a virtue.

When he eventually recovered, Ignatius walked all the way to Jerusalem, albeit on aching and damaged legs – not just once but twice, for the first time he was not received by monks in Jerusalem and was unceremoniously sent away. Perhaps, like Ignatius, my own hoped-for pilgrimage might happen far into the future. And perhaps, like him, I could do with making the inner journey to discover peace and contentment within. Reading and thinking might be not only a useful diversion, but a journey of a different kind. In my immediate situation, though, I felt closer to the bedridden and bored phase of his life, a parody of my former self. Hearing the phone ring or the post arrive, my mind would jump to attention, but it took two minutes to get out of the chair. At the sound of my son scampering down the stairs my heart would leap into action, but every answering movement was slow and painful.

Losing one's sense of humour is often a side effect of a painful illness and, realising this was happening to me, I thought of another literary figure who, when circumstance immobilised him, fought back with wit and satire. In 1790 Xavier de Maistre, locked in his room under house arrest for six weeks, made light of his temporary inconvenience and took it as an opportunity to think, read and contemplate. De Maistre (1763–1852) had been serving in Piedmont as an officer in the Sardinian army when he was arrested for duelling, and this lengthy isolation was his punishment. With only his dog and his servant for company, de Maistre walked about his room in his favourite pyjamas, imagining himself to be on a cultural journey and in the process constructing a parody of the travel writing of the time. His room was rectangular and of modest proportions, but he declared that he could not necessarily travel in a straight line; instead he took detours via the table or the armchair, pausing here and there to view his furniture, the engravings on the wall, the mirror and the view from the window as if they were the itinerary of a Grand Tour. With nothing to see apart from the ordinary objects in his room, it was as if he saw them for the first time and began to realise that a true engagement with the history of such ordinary objects, and the memories they summoned up, was just as capable of inspiring personal reflection and development as seeing the great wonders of the world. The mind and the soul are affected not so much by the relative beauty or grandeur of what is seen, but by the depth of engagement with it. Engaging the imagination is what leads to understanding the world, regardless of whether or not that is combined with an actual physical journey.

The travel writing of the time was much influenced by the Grand Tour – the journey made by young adults to expose them to the art, music and cultural finesse of Europe. Until the advent of the railways in the nineteenth century the Tour was mainly undertaken by wealthy and aristocratic youths, but – as with modern-day tourism – the impact of travel depends very much on the traveller's willingness to be exposed to new experiences. Just as a booze-and-clubbing trip to Ibiza does nothing to extend one's cultural borders, so it was possible for those making the Grand Tour, with their own cook, guide and valet, to be largely insulated from the impact of foreign culture. De Maistre's *Voyage autour de ma chambre* gently parodied the overblown quality of some travel writing and also demonstrated, with an elegantly light touch, that what matters is not where you go, but whether you pay attention to where you are. And he was as interested in the sheer pleasure of contemplation as in its value for the soul. 'There's no more attractive pleasure, in my view, than following one's ideas wherever they lead,' he wrote; and later, 'We should allow ourselves to laugh, or at least to smile, each time an innocent opportunity to do so presents itself.'

No matter how much I would have liked to follow de Maistre's recipe for a journey round my room, I was not in a light-hearted frame of mind. It was all very well telling myself that I could take a pilgrimage of the mind, but the truth was that my disappointment at the disintegration of my summer plans was a mere surface detail: what was really bothering me deep down was the fear that my body might never really work properly again. De Maistre at least knew that his imprisonment would end after forty days, but I was afraid I might be stuck here for ever. I couldn't just talk myself into a nice little mental retreat and pretend it was going to be fine.

Then I thought of Coleridge. A well-travelled man, he spent his early twenties exploring mainland Europe and later underwent great discomforts as he sailed to Malta to take up a position there. As a young man he was a devotee of enormously long walks, to the point of overdoing it – there are records of him walking as much as thirty miles in a day, and sometimes walking miles through the rain to visit Dorothy and William Wordsworth. Perhaps unsurprisingly, then, his writing often includes imaginary journeys over land or sea. But despite his exertions (and sometimes even because of them), Coleridge was somewhat given to ill health and at various point in his career his writing reflects this. One of his most beautiful poems, 'This Lime Tree Bower My Prison', came about through a moment of unwelcome immobility. Spending a weekend with friends, they had decided to take a long walk in the late spring sunshine, but Coleridge felt ill and decided not to join them on the walk. Deeply disappointed, he sat pensively beneath a lime tree regretting the loss of the company of his friends and of the store of memories he might have gained:

> Well, they are gone, and here must I remain,
> This lime-tree bower my prison . . .
> They, meanwhile,
> Friends, whom I never more may meet again,
> On springy heath, along the hill-top edge,
> Wander in gladness . . . [2]

In his mind's eye Coleridge imagined his friends encountering the beauty of trees, brooks, waterfalls and eventually the sight of the sea, sails glinting in the sunlight. Stuck at home, he was upset that he was missing such a treat, but worst of all he was missing their company, and in particular 'gentle-hearted Charles' (Charles Lamb), who lived in the city and, as Coleridge saw it, was desperate for what the countryside offered. Perhaps Coleridge imagined himself pointing out these beautiful sights, and perhaps also that his own company might have been a significant part of what Lamb had been longing for in his country retreat:

> . . . for thou hast pined
> And hunger'd after Nature, many a year,
> In the great City pent, winning thy way
> With sad yet patient soul, through evil and pain
> And strange calamity!

But then a change came over Coleridge, as he realised that his imagined journey had done him good. Not only that, but the opportunity for reflection made him realise that the ability to appreciate his surroundings depends not on the location itself, but on the attitude of mind. He could walk through beautiful countryside and not notice it at all. Or he could sit in his own garden and see things he'd never noticed before.

> A delight
> Comes sudden on my heart, and I am glad
> As I myself were there! Nor in this bower,

> This little lime-tree bower, have I not mark'd
> Much that has sooth'd me . . .

Finally he concludes:

> . . . sometimes
> 'Tis well to be bereft of promis'd good,
> That we may lift the soul, and contemplate
> With lively joy the joys we cannot share.

All of Coleridge's conversation poems follow this pattern – a journey outwards, then the climactic moment serves as a catalyst to change the lens through which everything is seen, and finally the poem winds its way back to its starting point which, in the light of the imagined journey, is now seen in a completely new perspective. Coleridge, like Dante before him, saw in the journey of the imagination something that goes beyond a change of mood or demeanour; there is here a genuine possibility for a complete change of mind, a moment of enlightenment after which nothing will ever be the same again.

Ignatius, de Maistre and Coleridge all seemed to be offering me the same piece of advice: I could read to distract and entertain myself until I was up and about again, or I could, through reading and through paying attention to the minutiae of life, embark on a real journey of the imagination. But the second option, judging by the wisdom of these literary and spiritual forebears, might turn out to be at least as strenuous as the walk I had planned for us to make through northern Spain. For the inner journey of pilgrimage is not so much about the destination itself as it is about sharpening one's sense of observation of oneself and one's surroundings. I do not need to go to Rome or Canterbury or walk the Camino to find inner rest and a new pace of life. What I need is to notice myself in my surroundings, in the present moment. I can't be a tourist by staying at home, but I might make a better pilgrimage in my own kitchen than by walking hundreds of miles, if this is where I learn to watch and listen to my own soul.

⟿

The journey inwards, as it happens, has a venerable history and is not unconnected to the early Christian idea of being a stranger and a pilgrim on the earth. Around the late third and early fourth centuries, well before the first Christian monasteries were founded, a trickle of Christian believers began to take the idea of being strangers and aliens to a very radical extreme, separating themselves from normal society completely. Leaving the large cosmopolitan cities of Rome and Alexandria, they withdrew into the desert regions of Sinai, Syria and Judea to pursue lives of solitude and asceticism. Some of the earliest of these Desert Fathers and Mothers were motivated in part by the need to flee terrible persecution, but once Constantine had made Christianity legal and it gradually became not only acceptable but socially advantageous to belong to the Church, another wave of believers retreated to the desert to avoid their faith being compromised by materialism and social ambition. With only the bare minimum of food, clothes and possessions, they spent their days in prayer and contemplation. Some were eremitic, or hermits (from the Greek *eremos*, meaning 'desert') and placed the emphasis on solitude. Others built coenobite communities (from the Greek *koinos* and *bios*, meaning 'common' and 'life') in which the community experience was a key factor, or skete communities which combined both features by encouraging some solitude within a community. John Cassian wrote his own thoughts on how to live the monastic life, and also recorded some conversations that he and his friend Germanus had with the Desert Fathers, and these were among the ideas that laid the foundations for later monasticism.

The Desert Fathers (and a few women, too, whose lives were recorded among the saints of the desert) saw solitude and deprivation as a way of preparing themselves for the heavenly city of God. The expectation that Jesus would soon return fuelled their sense of detachment from the concerns of this world and, far away from the distractions of secular life and the demands of physical appetite, their pure, ascetic lifestyle became a pilgrimage of a different kind: neither a counter-cultural route through everyday society, nor a physical journey to a sacred place, but an inner journey of faith. These hermits and coenobites took more literally than most the words of Jesus to the rich young ruler: 'Sell everything you have and give to the poor . . . Then come, follow me' (Luke 18:22).

The desert way of life was not regarded as spiritually superior, nor was it recommended for everyone, but it was seen as a calling and any wisdom gained by the Desert Fathers was shared with other Christians – those who remained involved in everyday society and theologians who were involved in councils, disputes and discussions as the young Church worked out its identity. Sometimes retreatants visited the Desert Fathers for short periods to sit under their teaching, and from time to time a hermit would leave the desert to visit Christians in the towns.

Anthony the Great, sometimes called 'the father of monks', set the example here. He went to live in complete solitude in the desert in about AD 285 and attracted plenty of followers. After twenty years in the desert, he left his hermitage to act as spiritual father to a group of coenobites. Five years later he again retreated into solitude, where he remained until he died at the grand old age of 105 – except for two occasions when he visited Alexandria, once to encourage Christians who were under persecution there, and again in 338 when Athanasius called on Anthony to help him stand up to the heretical teachings of Arius – thereby making clear through his actions that pilgrimage is not just for the pilgrim, but for the wider world, for the 'other'.

Athanasius, who was a theologian, wrote a biography of Anthony which includes accounts of him being attacked by demons who tried to distract him from his life of holiness.[3]

The silence of the wilderness, the lack of distractions and material possessions led the Desert Fathers to adopt a contemplative form of prayer. Once a young acolyte of Abba Peter asked the old man to teach him the secret of prayer.

'Do you have a book of the Psalms?' said the old man. 'And is there a particular Psalm you are fond of?'

'I do, Abba,' said the young man.

'And is there one verse of that Psalm that you know and love?'

'Yes, there is,' came the reply.

'Then use that one verse as your prayer,' said Abba Peter.

The young man was puzzled, thinking that it would take only minutes to recite such a short prayer, and asked how long this prayer should take.

'Pray it for an hour,' said Abba Peter.

An hour later the disciple returned and asked what he should do next.

'Pray your verse all day,' said Abba Peter, 'and return tomorrow.'

The young man prayed all day, and when he returned the next day he couldn't believe his ears when he was told to continue to pray the same single verse for a whole week. But, having chosen Abba Peter as his guide, he persevered with the prayer.

After a week he approached Abba Peter and pleaded with him to be able to keep the same prayer for a while longer.

The old man smiled. 'If you really want to learn the secret of prayer, it will be enough for you to continue with this prayer for your entire life,' he said.

The sayings of the Desert Fathers can in some places seem fantastic and unbelievable to the twenty-first-century reader, but amidst the graphic descriptions of their struggles with demons and visitations from angels, there are elements of their spiritual quest that have a timeless quality. Their teachings eventually became the inspiration for Western monasticism, Anglo-Saxon saints such as Cuthbert and Guthlac, and the late medieval anchorites.

The idea of an inner journey was not a new one to me. In the course of my life I have been on a number of different retreats, sometimes in a group and a few times in complete silence and solitude. Depending on your preconceptions and your personality, a retreat can sound like a blissful or a dire experience. The truth, I have discovered, is that they can turn out either way. The first time I was persuaded to go on a retreat it was an absolute disaster, and I came to the conclusion that the man who led it had no idea what he was doing. He insisted, once we arrived, that the members of the group should make a complete fast for the first twenty-four hours, and despite the unwillingness of two members of the group to undertake such a fast, he said that if we didn't go on this journey together it wouldn't work. So fast we did, and by the end of the day I had such a splitting headache that I spent the next twenty-four hours in bed and missed the rest of the exercise. After that I avoided retreats for a long time, until much later someone persuaded me to visit a monastic community deep in the countryside of northern England. 'Honestly,' she said, 'this place is nothing like the creepy old institutions you're imagining. The Brothers and Sisters are delightful, the house and gardens are stunningly beautiful, and they take very seriously the monastic tradition of treating their guests well. Peace, quiet, time to think and rest and pray – what's not to like?'

My friend's warm recommendation persuaded me to sign up for a five-day visit, but even so I wasn't entirely sure I was doing the right thing. What if they expected me to pray eight hours a day? What if I didn't understand the rules? What if everything was in Latin? I almost cancelled at the last moment, but then decided I might as well go and check it out. After all, they weren't going to lock me in, and if I hated it I could just leave.

As I drove up to the gates of the abbey the high walls that surrounded the grounds looked somewhat forbidding and underscored every fear and negative preconception I had of religious communities. I took a few deep breaths before driving through the huge gates and parked the car. Once inside, though, I was struck by the peacefulness and order in the neatly kept gardens, and in the distance I could see two black-robed monks trimming a hedge. I walked up to the huge front door and knocked.

After a few minutes the door creaked open and there stood a small, bearded monk with an enormous smile. As he welcomed me inside he enquired about my journey, pointed out a few features of the building and commented on the weather report and something in the news. He seemed far more normal than I had expected, speaking English in the vernacular and seeming quite connected to the real world. I breathed a little easier. Then I was introduced to the young Brother whose job it was to take care of the guests that week. Brother Richard gave me a quick tour of the gardens, the library and the chapel, and then walked me over to the guest house. He carried my luggage up to my room and as we climbed the stairs he explained the time-table of the community, and said that I should go to the dining hall for meals when the bell rang.

'If you miss dinner, there are a few snacks in the fridge – just help yourself,' he said. 'Right now, though, why not take a rest? You look tired.'

'Thank you,' I said, appreciating the kind thought but noting to myself that he clearly didn't understand that I wasn't the kind of person who has a lie down in the middle of the day. 'I guess I'm a bit tired from the journey. I'll relax for a bit. But after that, would it be OK if I go back to that library and do some reading?'

Brother Richard looked at me intently. 'No, I don't think so,' he said. 'It's not that we don't allow guests into the library. It's just that from your letter, it sounds as if you've been working too hard lately. And reading isn't leisure, it's work.'

'Well, I'll just look at the maps I've brought, then,' I said. 'The countryside round here is fantastic and I might do a walk tomorrow.'

'I would suggest not,' he said calmly. 'We do encourage our guests to go on walks. But walking more than a mile or so would be tiring. If you've been working too hard, you need to rest. Walk in the gardens instead – that's enough to stretch your legs and get some fresh air without tiring yourself out.'

Two thoughts were now bouncing round my brain: first, that I must look shockingly tired, and second, that I seemed not to have anything to do for five whole days. No phone, no entertainment, no books, no walks . . . how was I going to fill up the days? But wait – he hadn't given me the spiritual instructions yet. No doubt he would order me to spend hours praying and poring over the Bible. I felt the car key in my pocket, reminding myself that I was here by choice and if it got weird I could leave.

But Brother Richard said nothing about praying, and gave me a twinkly smile as he turned to leave. 'See you at dinner,' he said. His black habit swished out of sight, but a second later he reappeared in the doorway.

'Oh, and by the way,' he added, 'don't even think about praying for hours on end. There's really no need for you to pray much at all while you're here. We are praying for you, so you can just relax. That's why you are here.'

This was nothing like the punishing religion I'd been expecting. I had never in my life before been told *not* to pray! Was it possible, perhaps, that behind the grim features of a God for whom nothing would ever be enough, there might be a way of encountering something that was just pure goodness? I threw my car keys into the back of the drawer, stretched out on the bed and decided to stay and find out.

A couple of hours later I met Brother Richard on the pathway, walking towards the dining room. 'We eat in silence,' he said, 'but don't worry, people will pass everything to you. It will probably seem a bit unusual if you've never done it before.'

No kidding. Total silence?

When we arrived in the dining room, a tiny bird-like woman materialised at my side, smiled broadly and indicated that I should follow her. It wasn't until I actually sat down that I realised that when you stop speaking all the other habits of normal society suddenly don't work any more. Good manners, as I had imbibed them, involve ensuring that you don't simply treat people as vehicles for your own wishes: if you ask them to pass the salt, you don't then ignore them and disappear behind the newspaper. I guess it's back to the company thing – eating together is more than just getting food; it's about meeting the people you eat with. But with permission to speak removed, suddenly looking directly at another person feels all out of place. How do you 'meet' people and communicate with them if you don't speak?

I was pleasantly surprised to discover that this little community had mastered the art of eating in silence, and that – done well – it can actually even heighten the sense of good manners and meeting the other person. To start with, the members of the community were not being silent just for the sake of it. The silence had a purpose: it avoided the tiring kind of small talk that you have to make when what you really need is to eat a little and rest a little without breaking up the flow of the working day. And the silence was creatively used because, following St Benedict's Rule,[4] one member of the community read to everyone else from the book of the week. It wasn't a dreary religious book, either – it was one of the recent political autobiographies, and over the course of the five days I heard all of it read out loud, like a live audiobook.

The community had perfected the art of silent table manners. I didn't have time to wonder whether I might need a little salt on my vegetables before the salt was placed in front of me. Moments later the butter appeared beside my plate. Looking up and down the table I saw the community, while listening intently to their book, looking round at each other's plates and passing water, butter, salt and pepper as it seemed to be required. It took a few meals to get the hang of it and stop feeling self-conscious. But then the restfulness of it took over. How wonderful not to have to do mindless chit-chat, not to have to wait through someone's endless monologue before feeling it appropriate to ask for the water.

The same nun who took such great care of me at every mealtime also appeared at my side, as if by magic, each evening at the service of sung Compline, and I was aware that she was keeping an eagle eye out just in case I got lost and didn't know when to sit or stand, speak or sing. Towards the end of the week I wanted to thank her for looking out for me, but I wasn't sure when would be the right moment in the day to speak to her. I asked Brother Richard for advice.

'Actually, you can't speak to her,' he said. 'She is one of the few here who lives entirely in silence.'

I could barely believe my ears, but this one piece of information changed my understanding of human relationships. I can honestly say that I have never felt more attention being paid to me than I have by that tiny nun, with whom I never exchanged even a single word, and the last time I saw her before leaving the monastery I smiled at her, hoping she might understand my wordless thanks. She clasped my hands between hers, smiling and gazing into my eyes, with a depth of care and love that is rare to behold. Clearly this amazing nun had completely internalised the two great hallmarks of Benedict's Rule: silence and hospitality. I was being treated as if I was the most important person in the world – literally so, for Benedictines are taught to receive their guests as if it was Jesus himself who walked in. 'Let all guests who arrive be received like Christ . . . for He is going to say, "I came as a guest, and you received Me" (Matt. 25:35). And to all let due honour be shown, especially . . . to pilgrims.'[5]

One day Brother Richard informed me that he was soon to go to visit a family member who was seriously ill. The abbot had granted him leave to travel, and when the day came he would put on normal clothes and leave the priory. We talked for a while about the relationship between physical stillness and contemplation, and in conversation we also discovered that we had a mutual friend, a man who at that time was seeking to join a monastic order himself. Brother Richard laughed. 'He'll have no trouble with chastity or obedience,' he said, 'but stability? No way. He can't sit still long enough to be a Benedictine monk. He would do better as a Friar, staying more closely connected to the world and able to travel about. No one should join an order unless it suits them – you have to have certain inclinations for it to work. For the right person it's a massive freedom. For anyone else it would stifle them.'

The vow of stability is the anchor by which Benedictines live: it doesn't mean they never travel – far from it – but it does mean that they take very seriously being rooted within their community. Like the desert hermits and coenobites, their voluntary exile from everyday society frees them to focus on an inward, contemplative journey. This is not, however, a self-absorbed, navel-gazing exercise; instead the objective is to integrate the self before God and to learn to pay close attention to others. This is helped by the vow of obedience, which may sound unnecessarily authoritarian to the modern ear, but at the abbey I learned that the word 'obedience' came from two Latin words, *ob*, meaning 'to', and *audire*, meaning 'listen'. The very first word in the Rule of St Benedict is 'Listen'. Obedience in this sense has to do with paying attention, listening closely to God, to your own heart and to those around you. Benedict's Rule suggests that this quality of listening is hard work and takes place in relationship with others. Seeking the guidance of the abbot is one way the Brothers and Sisters learn to listen, but there is a mutuality to this relationship too, for the Rule instructs the abbot to listen to them too, to pay special attention to the youngest and newest member of the community and not assume that a novice's opinions are worth nothing. The attentive listening of this *ob-audire* obedience (if it's done in the right way) is not a strange sacrifice of personal autonomy, but a call to a depth of human relationship that would equally be at home in a family context. Parents who pay close attention to their kids and listen to their point of view are likely to have happier homes than those who beat their kids into submission. Any system has the potential to become a twisted parody of itself, and the horror stories told by those who have survived cruelty and abuse in monasteries serve as a warning that obedience should never be blind. Nevertheless, it was an education to see at first hand a community where obedience as close listening had created a security and warmth of relationship that was the very opposite of a punishing authoritarianism.

⇒

Monastics, like the Desert Fathers before them, choose an unusual way of life that is not easy and should only be undertaken by those who will flourish under its conditions. Like many outsiders to such a culture, I had assumed that monasteries are harsh and unforgiving and had been pleasantly surprised to discover first hand that, at its best, monastic life is marked by kindness, gentleness and respect.

There's a story about a hunter who went into the desert and unexpectedly came across Anthony the Great and his coenobitic community. The hunter had heard of the harsh asceticism of the Desert Saints, and so he was shocked to find Anthony's community eating, drinking wine and laughing together, not matching up to his expectations at all.

Anthony walked a short distance with the hunter and then told him to put an arrow in his bow and shoot into the air. The hunter shot an arrow. 'Shoot another,' said Anthony, and the hunter did as he was asked. Then Anthony asked him to shoot another arrow, and this time the hunter objected: 'If I bend my bow too much it will break.'

'It's the same with the work of God,' said Anthony. 'If we stretch people beyond their capacity, they will break too. Sometimes it's necessary to meet their human needs.'

Everywhere you look there are stories about how religion has harmed people: too many terrible accounts of cruelty and abuse that have occurred in churches and religious communities. It's completely illogical to draw the conclusion that all religion is harmful, but it's perhaps not surprising that both monastic life and pilgrimage have had as many critics as admirers. And one critique that has been levelled at each of them from time to time is that they are running away from something.

A thousand years after the first monasteries were established, medieval pilgrimages, both for lay and religious pilgrims, had become as much a leisure pursuit as a form of penance – a journey for curiosity, for breaking the routine of a dull life, for business pursuits and social pleasures. The early Reformers took a dim view of these medieval tourists, fearing that pilgrimage was either an excuse for self-indulgence, or a means of running away from difficulties or responsibilities. Among the first to denounce them were the Lollards, a Puritan group who regarded pilgrimages as a waste of money and an opportunity for sinful pleasures, who believed that people would live out their religion better by staying at home and taking care of their responsibilities. Their views were echoed by leading reformer Martin Luther, who, more than a hundred years after Chaucer wrote his *Canterbury Tales*, spoke disparagingly of pilgrimage. Luther was widely known for objecting to the way the Church abused people's credulity to extract money from them. More than a few lavish buildings were financed through the sale of pardons and indulgences, both in local churches and at pilgrimage destinations, and Luther campaigned against the Church's encouragement of pilgrimage. But he also criticised the hedonistic motives of the pilgrims themselves. If you really wanted to find God, Luther said, you would do better to find him by staying at home and fulfilling your responsibilities than by gadding about on trips abroad.

In 1520 Luther wrote, 'All pilgrimages should be stopped. There is no good in them: no commandment enjoins them, no obedience attaches to them. Rather do these pilgrimages give countless occasions to commit sin and to despise God's commandments.'[6] There is nothing to suggest that Luther lacked a sense of humour, or objected to people enjoying themselves – he liked singing and enjoyed family life. His objections to pilgrimage were due to his dismay that pilgrimage led people to devalue the places in which they actually lived, it upset him to see them being impoverished through superstition, and he wanted to free people from the burden of believing that God's favour could be earned through penitential acts and restore to them the truth that grace is a gift from God, received by faith alone.

Luther's point is a good one: if pilgrimage, or any other religious practice, descends into a superstitious act, then it does need to be reformed. But was he right that pilgrimage was just a means of avoiding the difficulties of 'real' life? And – more pertinent to me – if I embarked on an armchair pilgrimage, would my inner journey of the imagination be something of value, or would I be merely distracting myself from real life?

There are numerous stories in the Bible about people who run away – some to escape from danger and others to evade responsibilities. These tales cover the sense of panic and desperation of people in danger, the relief of finding a place of safety, the overwhelming emotion of those who eventually come back home again, a careering comedy or two where people are in reality running away from themselves, and some poignant poetry when they eventually make peace with their own lives. In most cases their journeys end up reinforcing the idea that you can't run away from yourself, or from God.

One of the funniest of these is the book of Jonah, a tale of an ordinary and intelligent man who had a bit of a chip on his shoulder. To get the best out of Jonah you need to abandon any idea of a preacher in a pulpit, and instead tune in to a slapstick comedy with the poignant tears-of-a-clown overtones of comedians like Laurel and Hardy. Everything Jonah attempted was designed for success, but went woefully, hopelessly wrong – hence the slapstick. But you can also feel some sympathy with Jonah, because it's clear that deep down he knew right from the start that his harebrained schemes were doomed and the outcome of the story, which he was trying to avoid, was inevitable.

The story begins with Jonah hearing of a city where the inhabitants' lifestyle was so utterly dissolute that they failed to notice that their entire society was about to go down the drain. He believed himself to be called by God to go and set them right – but he didn't want to. Why? Because Jonah knew that God was kind, merciful and forgiving. In his view, God was a bit of a pushover for the penitent. So Jonah rejected his calling and instead boarded a ship sailing in the opposite direction. The sequence of events that follows is hilarious: first there's a storm at sea that nearly kills them all, then he claims that the storm is his fault and his fellow sailors throw him overboard. He's swallowed by a huge fish, who later vomits him up onto dry land. Only then does he give in. (I can imagine Oliver Hardy as God here, and Stan Laurel as Jonah, his little face crumpling as he goes off to Nineveh as he should have done in the first place.) He then goes and denounces the city's dissolute living, they mend their ways and are eternally grateful for the heads up, while Jonah, who wanted some fire and brimstone from God, is furious because, just as he predicted, God has been kind and forgiving. Jonah goes and takes out his anger on a nearby sunflower, the equivalent, more or less, of kicking the cat.

A few pages away from this comic story is Psalm 139, a thoughtful song lyric by an author who sounds like he knew something about the impulse to run away. 'Where can I go from your Spirit?' the psalmist asks God. 'Where can I flee from your presence?' His words are most often quoted as a reassurance of God's omnipresence and omniscience, but they read to me more like an account of someone who has only just stopped running, only just given in to the inevitable. 'You hem me in behind and before . . . If I rise on the wings of the dawn, if I settle on the far side of the sea, even there your hand will guide me.'

Journeys, both real and imaginary, can be a way of running away, but they can equally be a means of transformation. When Thomas Cook first set up his travel company, his idea was that introducing people to what was unfamiliar abroad would transform their experience of life at home. But the unfamiliar can also be encountered through reading and other media. Just as travellers can choose to step outside their comfort zone, so can readers and listeners.

Centuries earlier, in his *Divine Comedy*, Dante captured something of this necessary journey of the imagination. He wrote in an era in which travel literature was – even more extremely than today – overlaid with fantasy and fiction, but this resulted, in a way, in the travel literature limiting itself to the conventions of its own time and place, rather than making a genuine connection with the unfamiliar. Dante, on the other hand, was deliberately using an imagined journey through hell, purgatory and paradise as an allegory of the spiritual journey, but was clear that if the mind was to make a pilgrimage it could only do so by engaging with the unfamiliar. Of all the real-life pilgrims Dante had encountered, the ones who impressed him were the ones who, passing through Florence on their way to Rome, allowed themselves to be steeped in the experience of an unfamiliar culture – the medieval equivalent of the modern traveller who eschews the comfort of the familiar, the Holiday Inn, the ubiquitous Starbucks and McDonald's – and instead stays with a local family who don't speak his/her language and who serve up unrecognisable coffee and unfamiliar food.

Years ago I travelled through Greece and what was then Yugoslavia. One morning after an early walk through stunningly beautiful countryside I stopped in a small village for breakfast. My thoughts turned to a good cup of coffee – which for me meant a tall mug of filter coffee, milk and no sugar. There was no café in sight, so my friend and I went into the local bakery. Behind the counter stood a tiny woman, brown and wrinkled from years of sun and dressed in black from head to toe. With only rudimentary Greek at our disposal, we asked where a café might be found. She frowned a little, peered at us for a moment, and then her face lit up with mirth as she smiled broadly. Waving her hands at us, she disappeared behind the shop. There were sounds of clattering and furniture scraping on the floor, and eventually she returned and waved us through to her own kitchen. Evidently there was no café in the village, but there was a tradition of hospitality for strangers that we had not encountered before.

We sat for about twenty minutes as she poured beans into a hand-grinder, boiled up water in a tiny little saucepan no bigger than a tea cup, and then poured in coffee grounds and sugar in roughly equal quantities. Eventually two enormous glasses of cold water appeared on the table, followed by plates of very dry, biscuity pastries, and two tiny cups of the strongest, blackest coffee I had ever seen. After a few sips I felt an immediate and extreme caffeine buzz and understood instantly why this coffee was served with a pint of water on the side. By now conversation had completely ground to a halt, and the only way we could communicate was through sign language and by pointing at pictures and maps to indicate where we were going. She regaled us with a lecture of which we understood not a single word, but it seemed she thought there was something ill-advised about our journey. The absurdity of this incomprehensible conversation mixed with the amazing caffeine high began to make us all laugh, but the real comedy moment came when I took another mouthful of coffee, only to discover that the bottom half of the cup was full of boiled coffee grounds: evidently you were only meant to take a few sips of the liquid from the top of the cup and leave the rest. Our tiny host was in peals of laughter by this time, as her two guests, clearly way out of their comfort zone, provided her with a morning's unexpected entertainment.

This is the kind of experience Dante associates with his favourite kind of pilgrim – the ones who will separate themselves from familiar surroundings, willing to look foolish in order to discover something new about the world, about God and about themselves. And he envisages a similar kind of launching into an alien environment.

He casts the mind itself as a pilgrim, travelling in its dream state into unknown territory. The intellectual game of demonstrating one's own knowledge or proving the superiority of one's own argument had to be abandoned: this was a search for self-knowledge that could only be gained by those willing to extend themselves, consciously, into a place where they had no knowledge, authority or expertise. In this state, Dante pictures himself (Canto 9, *Purgatorio*) standing at the door of purgatory, which is guarded by a huge angel with wings and a sword. He falls prostrate on the steps and begs the angel to let him in. But even once access is granted, the movement of entering into purgatory is still a struggle, and the huge, heavy doors open reluctantly, with the sound of metal grinding against stone. Crossing the threshold is not merely a matter of obtaining a ticket, but a struggle to move forward inch by inch, every step a step into the unknown (Canto 9, *Purgatorio*).

From Dante's point of view, then, whether you travel physically or in the mind, making yourself vulnerable to an alien setting is essential to personal growth. Travel might be nothing more than a holiday or a jaunt, a luxury we could do without; but there are times when simply leaving everything behind for a while enables you to return stronger and with renewed perspective on daily life. A good holiday can blow away the cobwebs, get you out of a rut, break the cycle of routine, restore balance, enable change and make you more productive. So – despite what Luther might have thought – there are many good reasons for believing that a purposeful trip away from home or a journey of the imagination might be the very opposite of running away, and ultimately will serve to make one a better citizen of life.

My armchair pilgrimage, I was clear, was not a matter of running away, denial, disappointment or any other escape mechanism. I wanted an interior journey that would not only keep me occupied while I was laid up, but would also give me a means of coming to terms with life as it was for me at that point, in the discomfort of the present moment and the uncertainty about the future.

For Xavier de Maistre the key was to pay the closest of attention to his everyday surroundings; to discover what he had failed to notice because of familiarity. For Dante the inner pilgrimage depended on using the imagination to stretch oneself outside what was familiar. For Ignatius, his pilgrimage began long before he regained his strength, still in convalescence, through close and contemplative reading. And for Coleridge, under his lime tree bower, it was both; the imaginative journey out was exactly what made him register what was right under his nose. With the wisdom of these literary heroes as an example, therefore, I decided to spend the summer reading, not in order to run away from my circumstances, but to see what an imaginative journey might do to transform them.

The subject of my armchair pilgrimage was an easy choice. There on the shelf was a row of books about walking the Camino, some I'd already read and a handful more I'd planned to take with me on the trip. I began by reading again through the history and traditions of the walk, from Aymeric Picaud's twelfth-century account to the classic guide by Elías Valiña Sampedro, one of the principal figures in the twentieth-century revival of the Camino pilgrimage, and then worked through a number of personal accounts of other people's walks and their experiences along the way. Like a good novel, a well-written memoir can transport the reader to another place, until you feel the heat on your back, the dust between your toes and the ache in your muscles. There is something quite incomparably wonderful about getting so lost in a book that you forget yourself, missing meals or staying awake into the early hours of the morning because you just have to find out what happens next. Reading about the Camino instead of walking it myself turned out not to be a poor substitute after all; every book I read was another step into the unfamiliar, the authors becoming like travelling companions, sharing their lessons in life.

The first of these was the one my friend Ben had written after walking all the way from Canterbury to Santiago with his trombone on his back.[7] *Pilgrim Snail* brought to mind my own slightly maverick pushchair pilgrimages. Ben's account was more travelogue than spiritual meditation and proved the perfect introduction to the Camino. His gently comical tales reminded me that even in the best of health, with all the optimism and confidence you could hope for, there is no insulation from the unexpected and no guarantee that life will pan out according to plan. Before he ever got to the Camino itself, Ben adapted his plans several times to fit around fellow travellers, friends who went to join him for a leg of the trip, or strangers he met along the way. Here and there was a hiatus in his journey when he fell in love, and his take on the Camino and the pilgrims he met there made me laugh. I relaxed as my anxieties unwound, and I began to hear, deep in my soul, a reminder of St Anthony's lesson for the hunter, or Brother Richard's instructions not to pray, for what this pilgrim needed right now was some help along the way. I climbed out of my usual mode of self-sufficiency and called friends in to help – with practical things, certainly, but more importantly, by helping me reconnect with hope and a sense of humour.

My second lesson came from Jennifer Lash's tale of her long journey through France and Spain, stopping at convents and shrines along the way.[8] She set out to reassess her own life after raising her kids and then surviving a severe illness, and her telling of the story of the journey was laced through with reflections on her life so far, and with moments at which her life had changed course and she had to let go of things she had held so dearly.

I found myself contemplating the idea of there being moments in life where it seems as if the road has unexpectedly been pushed into a diversion. We make much of choice in our culture, but most of us don't have quite as much power to choose as we'd like to believe – events take their own course and all we can do is adjust our view. I hadn't chosen my present situation, and it seemed to me I was taking 'the road less travelled',[9] not through virtue or vocation, but because life had dumped it on me.

Jennifer Lash's meditations brought me to see that as often as not what is laid before us isn't so much a choice between courses of action, but a challenge to renegotiate the future when life delivers us a set of unexpected circumstances. I didn't know at this stage what life would look like a few months down the track: whether I would get back to normal, or whether there would be a new version of normal. What was certain was that I couldn't go backwards.

Joyce Rupp's *Walk in a Relaxed Manner* was next on my pile of Camino books.[10] Again, for her the life-changing aspect of the pilgrimage proved to be the walk itself and the recurring theme of the book is neatly summed up in the title, for unlike the kind of Sunday afternoon stroll where you meander wherever the mood takes you, a pilgrimage is a long, planned walk. There's a daily ritual of checking the map, putting all your stuff in your backpack, lacing up your boots, checking you haven't left anything behind and then setting out on the next leg of the trip.

One of the important lessons of a long walk is that you have to find your own pace. Rupp described how, when younger and fitter people overtook her on the path, she felt the need to speed up and somehow prove that she was up to the task. Gradually she came to accept that her own pace was the right pace and that the purpose of her pilgrimage was not to complete a race, but to learn how to live. The same, she wrote, is true in life: illness, exhaustion, depression, irritability and a host of other demons can be exacerbated simply by failing to find a rhythm of life.

Walking has been my basic exercise all my life. For seven years I walked four miles a day to and from school, and weekends often involved an hour or two hiking out to a nearby forest, or sometimes a trip over to the Peak District for some more serious hills. But it wasn't until I was nineteen that I went on a really long walk. The summer of my first year at university, three friends and I set out to walk through the Lake District. The conditions were perfect: it was sunny but not too hot, and by using youth hostels we only needed to carry packs, not tents. But the flaw in the plan was that the walk was planned, and the hostels booked in advance, by the keenest and most experienced walker in the group. His theory was that by walking seventeen miles on the first day we would get to the perfect spot, from where the rest of the trip would fall beautifully into place. I thought about walking the Peaks, and estimated that this was going to be a full day. But I hadn't taken into account that this was seventeen miles up and down extremely steep hills. In the end we walked for eleven hours, and by the time we made it to the youth hostel we were very tired and the least experienced member of the group was beginning to get sore feet. 'Not to worry,' our trusty leader declared. 'It's a much easier walk tomorrow!' The girl with the sore feet said she was fine, and the next day we walked ten miles, and twelve the day after that. The third evening my feet were sore too – but that was nothing compared to the horrible mess that emerged when my friend took her socks off. She cried a lot, and I went to see the hostel manager to find out about transport. We discovered a minibus service called the Mountain Goat, which mostly operated to carry people's tents and luggage on ahead of them, leaving them free to walk without a heavy pack. But it also had room for a few passengers. On day four of our trip, two of us abandoned the walking and made a few days' journey by minibus, leaving the tougher walkers to scale Helvellyn on their own. The lesson I learned that year was that if you try too hard to keep up with people who have already established their own pace you can end up injured, stressed and immobilised.

By the time I read Joyce Rupp's account of the Camino, I had already several times been through a process of slowing myself down to a pace of life that is sustainable. It seems to be one of my inbuilt weaknesses to get too completely involved in the next project, the next piece of work, without planning in enough 'down time'. I get a lot done, but I sometimes put myself under too much pressure. And although focused hard work can be good in small doses, if it becomes a habit of life that you never break, it's bad for the soul as well as the body.

'What is life if, full of care, we have no time to stand and stare?' wrote William Henry Davies,[11] but though his words are often quoted life seems to have sped up even more since he wrote them. Our culture is addicted to doing everything faster than before: we have more time-saving appliances and gadgets than our grandparents ever dreamed of. But although speed and efficiency are good in the right place at the right time, it isn't good for everything to be wound up to fever pitch. It's too easy for life to become one long round of high-speed travel, instant downloads, texts, fast food, ready meals and eating on the run, and without realising it we lose the art of looking into someone's eyes and really listening to what they are saying. Carl Honoré called this 'the cult of speed', not just speeding up things that need to go faster, but winding up the whole of life until it's like a centrifuge that pins us to its revolutions.[12] Even our spirituality can be subject to this tendency towards speed and drivenness: the art of contemplation begins to feel like a waste of precious time. But spiritual growth is, by nature, something that only happens slowly.

Jesus told a parable about a farmer sowing seed on the land: some of it fell on the pathway and was eaten by birds, some fell on stony ground and didn't grow at all, some fell onto shallow soil and grew too fast, but was choked by weeds. Only the seed that disappeared into the ground and grew at the right speed produced a healthy crop.

Forced crops are usually deficient in trace elements; organic farmers will tell you that a crop that is fully nutritious has to grow at its natural pace. Like growing wheat, real spiritual growth has an optimum speed, and accelerating the growth and maximising the harvest will be about as much good for the soul as fast food is for the body. Some things just take time.

Maybe Jesus learned this little nugget of wisdom because he himself knew how to sit still and do nothing. Just before he told that parable, Matthew says Jesus was sitting on the beach. The Gospel writers often say that Jesus 'went out to pray' – sometimes all night in gardens or up mountains. But not on this occasion: 'Jesus went out of the house and sat beside the sea' (Matt. 13:1 NRSV). The parable of the sower is often preached as a message about evangelism. But given that he told the story to a crowd of people who interrupted him when he was taking time out, perhaps he had it more in mind that spiritual growth has nothing in common with the cult of speed. Right there in the Gospels is a mandate – should you need one – to do nothing from time to time.

❦

I continued through my pile of Camino books, some long and others short, some well written and others a bit lumpy in style, some deeply spiritual and others more amusing for their memoir quality. But one theme in particular began to emerge as a common thread. In almost every book I read there was an account of how each traveller had to stop at some point to reduce the amount of luggage they carried.

It's a familiar scene to anyone who has ever been on a walking holiday. You begin by trying to fit into your backpack all the things you need to take with you, but the priority quickly changes to working out what you can do without. In the first instance it's the sheer weight of the pack that forces a slimming down of the baggage, but after a while you discover a sense of freedom from simply not having all that stuff to keep an eye on.

Learning to cut down on the baggage has an impact when you get back home. Our lives are filled with too much stuff: the equipment and the decorations and the furniture for our houses, the photographs and books and files that we can't bear to part with yet never have time to sort out.

Much of what ties us to the earth is a burden of our own choosing, not a true obligation. Too much stuff (which then needs oiling and cleaning) ties us to our house on a weekend, when we might be following dragonflies along a riverbank, or chasing down kites, or climbing a hill, or cooking up a huge storm for a crowd of friends. Our homes serve many functions: they shelter us, welcome our friends, please us aesthetically, keep us warm, put a roof over our heads. But they shouldn't own us. Of course our personal history matters, and extreme minimalism isn't good for everyone. Nevertheless, being weighed down with too much paraphernalia that we no longer use or need is not a good place to be either. Choosing those things that matter and letting the rest go is a liberation; it makes a house easier to clean and cheaper to insure, and frees up time to get on with life.

Reading my way through one account after another of pilgrims who discovered a sense of lightness as they jettisoned baggage along the way, I found I was itching to lose some of the clutter that had accumulated in my life: possessions I no longer used or needed, clothes that lurked unworn at the back of the wardrobe, all the odds and ends that seem to multiply in the corners of the house when you're not looking. Moving around my house rather slowly and painfully, I had more time than usual to notice where the clutter had stacked up. I began to make a habit of picking up one or two things each day that were unused, unloved or unnecessary, and putting them in bags to be collected by the local charity vans. By the time autumn arrived I had two empty cupboards and I gave them away too.

As the space and light in my house increased, my spirits lifted. But something else interesting happened, for as I began to shed the weight of possessions I no longer wanted, I also started wanting to leave behind some bits of mental and emotional baggage I'd been carrying around. I've had a lot of good luck in my life, and a great deal to be thankful for, but I've also lived through a few bereavements and some crashing disappointments, each of which have left their scars. Talk flows easily from our lips about 'moving on', but in practice it's not all that easy to do and there were some griefs and sorrows that seemed to have wrapped their fingers round my heart and refused to let go.

Experience has taught me that putting down emotional baggage is easier to do in company, so I called on a long-time friend to help. It wasn't as though I hadn't talked about these things before, but this time there was a kind of ritual to the talking and listening. Saying things out loud is sometimes what's needed to make them concrete enough to put down and leave behind.

≈

Towards the end of the summer of my armchair pilgrimage, I looked back at what I'd learned since I stumbled accidentally into pilgrimage a few years earlier.

First, being a pilgrim isn't necessarily about being active. The opposite of being passive isn't moving about, but paying attention. Whenever there is an opportunity to see the world through someone else's eyes, and for the unfamiliar to cast its light on us, we have the choice to insulate ourselves against discomfort, or to pay attention and open ourselves up to what is new.

Second, a pilgrim isn't a meek, obedient do-gooder. From time to time I caught an echo in my mind of a song we used to sing in school assemblies when I was a child: 'He who would valiant be, 'gainst all disaster . . .' Singing to a rather out-of-tune piano in a lamentable, damp school hall felt a million miles away from anything adventurous or noble, but whenever I think of the song, I hear it in my mind being sung by a couple of hundred children's voices.

> There's no discouragement,
> shall make him once relent
> his first avowed intent
> to be a pilgrim.

It was a great tune, but I think that as a child I imbibed the idea that to be a pilgrim required a determined, unflinching commitment to reach a destination you hadn't chosen and that even a moment's discouragement or doubt would be a cause for guilt. The sense of Edwardian militaristic heroism that insisted we obediently 'follow the Master' seemed to suggest that the kind of small girl I was could never be a pilgrim. I wasn't deliberately disobedient, but I was particularly prone to losing track of time by burying myself in a good book or a piece of music, and I was never satisfied with an easy answer and asked far too many questions. I might have caught the pilgrim vision sooner had I known that the hymn was adapted from the far more gutsy, anti-authoritarian words of John Bunyan's *Pilgrim's Progress*, written while he was serving a prison sentence for preaching his passionate and unconstitutional beliefs. Bunyan never mentions following the Master at all, but wages war against hobgoblins, which might have been more appealing to the imagination of an eight-year-old. Even in adulthood it still took some effort to throw off the idea that being a pilgrim meant obedience to a dogmatic but unimaginative way of life. But real-life pilgrims, Bunyan included, were a fiery lot and to follow in their footsteps requires a sense of adventure, the ability to adapt to all kinds of circumstances and the willingness to be changed in heart, mind and soul.

The willingness to change, though, is balanced by knowing what you're looking for, and at this point in my explorations of pilgrimage I'm still wondering at the relationship between these two.

A well-known Celtic saying about pilgrimage suggests that pilgrimage itself doesn't guarantee an encounter with God:

> To go to Rome
> Is much trouble, little profit.
> The King whom thou seekest there,
> Unless thou bring Him with thee, thou wilt not find.[13]

There is undoubtedly some truth in this: what we seek is to some extent influenced by what we expect to find. But it's also true that to find God at all involves letting go of a domesticated vision of God and allowing the discomforts of unfamiliar and temporary surroundings to open us up to the possibility of being surprised by him. To 'bring him with thee' does not, I think, mean clinging to a watertight set of doctrines and beliefs that will be untarnished by experience. To seek God at all suggests that we have not yet reached our goal; to search for something implies that there is yet more to be found. I like Dante's image of entering into the knowledge of God only with a struggle that's akin to opening an old, jammed door that scrapes painfully against the doorstep. The knowledge of God that we do bring with us might propel us into searching for more, but the likelihood is that whatever we bring with us will have to be put down at some point, because whatever we think we know of God at any point is always provisional, always incomplete, always contingent. Any kind of pilgrimage, then, requires a delicate balance between knowing what we're looking for and the willingness to be completely disarmed by what we find.

For me there was, perhaps, a touch of irony in falling accidentally into pilgrimage only just at a point in my life when circumstances began to limit my freedom to travel. As a result it seemed to me that even as I was learning the rules, I was rewriting them. But I have come to the realisation that pilgrims have always rewritten the rules. The impulse to travel and the urge to find transformation have collided in different ways, so that a great patchwork of interpretations has given shape to the idea of pilgrimage both as a journey to illuminate life and as a journey through life itself. Abraham, Jonah, Helena and Brendan needed to make actual, physical journeys to find the key to life, The Desert Fathers and monastics chose the wilderness, while Luther called people simply to stay exactly where they were. St Paul spent his life travelling, but preached that the true journey was in another dimension. But of all the examples available to us to follow, and of all the writers who have left a record of their own pilgrimage, none of them suggests that we should merely follow their instructions; each one has also left us a mandate to break with convention and reinvent pilgrimage just as they did.

Whether inspiration comes from the reckless adventures of the *peregrini*, Helena's concern for historical connection to place, the lateral, imaginative vision of a poet, or the solitary pursuit of a hermit, the common thread is that every kind of pilgrimage pushes us into uncharted territory, either mentally or physically, and the end result is a transformation of a kind we couldn't have anticipated. In the end, whether by accident or on purpose, it's not where you go but who you become that makes you a pilgrim.

Notes

Chapter 1

1. *Itinerary from Bordeaux to Palestine, 'The Bordeaux Pilgrim' (ad 333)*, trans. Aubrey Stewart, annotated C.W. Wilson, Palestine Pilgrims' Text Society, London, 1887.

2. A 533-metre tunnel dug during the reign of Hezekiah (c. eighth century BC) when Jerusalem came under the threat of siege. The geography of the city was a good situation from the point of view of military defence, but its main water source, the Gihon Spring, lay outside the city walls. The tunnel was built to divert the water from the spring to a reservoir inside the city called the Pool of Siloam, and its construction is documented in 2 Kings 20:20 and 2 Chronicles 32:2–4, 30.

3. From the General Prologue to *The Canterbury Tales*. Chaucer began writing his *Tales* in 1387, 217 years after Becket's murder, when the popularity of pilgrimage to Canterbury was at its height. He died on 25 October 1400, with the *Tales* unfinished. The pilgrimage had, for many, become more a

form of leisure than a form of penance, and Puritan groups such as the Lollards viewed it as a waste of money and an excuse for riotous living.

4. *Pilgrims and Pilgrimage: Journey, Spirituality and Daily Life through the Centuries*, DVD-ROM, Christianity and Culture Series, University of York, 2003.

Chapter 2

1. Studies by Sir Ifor Williams, ed. Rachel Bromwich, *The Beginnings of Welsh Poetry*, Amsterdam: North-Holland Publishing Company, 1980, p. 102.

2. Sir Walter Scott, *Marmion*, 1808, Canto Second, IX.

3. St Aidan's Prayer for the Holy Island of Lindisfarne, Northumbria Community, Evening Prayer, Day 16.

4. Michel de Montaigne, *The Essays* (*Les Essais*), Book III, ch. 13, Paris: Abel Langelier, 1588.

5. Carved by Fenwick Lawson.

6. See, for instance, 1 Thessalonians 4:13–17; 2 Peter 3:13; Romans 8:19–20; Revelation 21:1–4.

7. Letter to Diognetus, ch. 5, A Roberts and J. Donaldson, *The Apostolic Fathers: Ante Nicene Christian Library Translations of the Writings of the Fathers Down to AD 325 Part One*, Whitefish: Kessinger Publishing, 2004. This letter is variously dated at about AD 130, or approximately AD 200, or later into the third century. It is uncertain who Diognetus was, but it's thought unlikely he was the same Diognetus who was a tutor of the Emperor Marcus Aurelius.

8. St Caecilius Cyprian, *The Treatises, VII, On Mortality*, 26.

9. Augustine, *Concerning the City of God against the Pagans*, Book XVIII: 54.

10. Irenaeus, *Adversus Haereses (Against the Heresies)*, 4.34.5–7.

11. *Peregrinus*, interestingly, is the Latin translation of *pároikos*, which has a double meaning. In Hellenistic Greek the verb *paroikéin* means to live nearby – to be a neighbour – and etymologically is the derivation of our word 'parish'. But it also came to be used for someone who lived as a foreigner in a country where they held no rights of citizenship. The Old Testament, in the Septuagint, usually takes this second meaning, so Abraham as a foreigner in Egypt was a *pároikos* (Gen. 12:10), and Joseph's brothers seeking food in Egypt were, as a group, *paroikía*. The New Testament generally uses this alternative meaning, so Jesus in Luke 24:18 is a stranger or a foreigner. And while the Church, in relationship to God, was *ekklēsia*, those who are called, in relationship to the world they were *paroikía*, foreigners, because they had in effect no passport or identity papers for earth, being citizens of heaven (Heb. 12:13).

12. Dante, *La Vita Nuova*, xii.

13. Robert Louis Stevenson, *Virginibus Puerisque*, 1881.

14. Christopher John Wright, *A Guide to the Pilgrims' Way*, London: Constable & Co., 1971.

Chapter 3

1. *The Pilgrims Guide* was written probably around 1140–50. An abridged translation appears in T.A. Layton, *The Way of St James or the Pilgrims' Road to Santiago*, London: Allen & Unwin, 1976.

2. Samuel Taylor Coleridge, 'This Lime Tree Bower My Prison', J.C.C. Mays (ed.), *The Collected Works of Samuel Taylor Coleridge: Poetical Works*, 1, vol. 1.1, Princeton: Princeton University Press, 2001.

3. Athanasius of Alexandria, *Life of Antony*, 3, in *Early Christian Lives*, trans. Carolinne White, London: Penguin Books, 1998. See also Benedicta Ward, *The Desert Fathers: Sayings of the Early Christian Monks*, London: Penguin Classics, 2003.

4. Each monastic order lives by a rule of life. The Rule of St Benedict, who died around AD 547, sets out in detail how each community is to be ordered. It is strict but not punishing, laying out principles for everything from the authority structure of the community to the daily allowance of bread, food and wine each monk should be given.

5. Rule of St Benedict, ch. 53.

6. Martin Luther, 'Address to the Christian Nobility', *Twenty-Seven Articles*, 1520, Part 1:12.

7. Ben Nimmo, *Pilgrim Snail: Busking to Santiago*, London: Flamingo, 2001.

8. Jennifer Lash, *On Pilgrimage*, London: Bloomsbury Publishing PLC, 1999.

9. Robert Frost, 'The Road Not Taken', from *Mountain Interval*, H. Holt and Co., 1916.

10. J. Rupp, *Walk in a Relaxed Manner*, New York: Orbis Books, 2005.

11. William H. Davies, 'Leisure', 1911.

12. Carl Honoré, *In Praise of Slow*, London: Orion, 2004.

13. Bernard and Atkinson, *The Irish Liber Hymnorum*, Henry Bradshaw Society, 1898.

Do you wish this wasn't the end?
Are you hungry for more great teaching, inspiring
testimonies, ideas to challenge your faith?

Join us at www.hodderfaith.com, follow us on Twitter
or find us on Facebook to make sure you get the latest from
your favourite authors.

Including interviews, videos, articles, competitions
and opportunities to tell us just what you thought about
our latest releases.

www.hodderfaith.com

 HodderFaith

 @HodderFaith

 HodderFaithVideo

HODDER
WHERE FAITH IS INSPIRED